Final Curtain Call

Rebamac

Colorful Crow Publishing

Published by

Colorful Crow Publishing

96 Craig Street Suite112-304 Ellijay, Georgia

http://www.colorfulcrowpublishing.com

©2024 by Rita McAlister

All rights reserved

Published in the United States of America

This is a work of fiction. While, as in all fiction, the literary perceptions and insights are based on experience, all names, characters, places, and incidents either are products of the author's imagination or are used fictitiously. No reference to any real person is intended or should be inferred.

ISBN (paperback) 978-1-964271-11-8

ISBN (e-book) 978-1-964271-12-5

Colorful Crow is committed to publishing works of quality and integrity. In that spirit, we are proud to offer this book to our readers; however, the story, the experiences, and the words are the author's alone.

To my two WONDERFUL children, my reasons for living.

For you are my hiding place; you protect me from trouble,
You surround me with songs of victory.
Psalm 32:7

One

It had been many lonely years since I had made my way back to the old home place where I grew up. But on this particular morning I felt an urgency to return there. It was shortly after I began my day with my coffee in hand that I received the news. I hurriedly gathered my keys and purse as I headed out the door. An hour's drive from my present home, I drove with such mixed emotions. Every muscle in my body tense, tears uncontrollably streaming down my face, my mind cluttered and my heart racing. But "why," questions flashed through my memory as I searched for a good answer. But there was not even one. The urgency and essence grew stronger within me as I longed to arrive at my safe place. I would often in my younger years retreat there and spend endless hours dreaming and contemplating what my future held. It was a place where all my dreams seemed to be within reach, at that moment anyway.

With the news received today, I needed to feel the serenity that my safe place offered me as a child. Returning to the terrace, now a green oasis overlooking the remains of what was once my home, I wept. Seen through the nostalgic eyes of my younger self, the transformation was heartbreaking. Time and nature had slowly but relentlessly taken over, leaving my childhood abode in a state of decay. The house, now distant and desolate, wore its abandonment openly. Its paint, now cracked and flaking, seemed to vanish into the wind, bit by bit. An occasional, prolonged creak from the porch's screen door broke the silence, swinging open and slamming shut at the whim of the wind—a mournful echo of solitude, as if the structure itself reminisced over the joy that once filled its spaces. The barn, too, was a shell of its former self, partially collapsed, succumbing to time's relentless march. The entire farm, once alive with the laughter of children and calls for dinner, now lay silent and forsaken.

The overgrown acreage resembled a ghost town, dust and tumbleweed the only residents. No one lived there anymore except in my memories of the days long since gone. I cleared a spot amidst the overgrown grass at the edge of the terrace and sat down in my time-worn yet familiar spot, elevated above the surroundings. Embracing the warmth of the sun on my face and the wind as it sent a swift release of a welcomed breeze. Even though the climb to the terrace was much more difficult than in my younger days, I loved it there. I always had. As I sat and traveled back to the memory of happier days with family and unfulfilled dreams, I realized that the dreams of sixty-odd years ago did not resemble any form or fashion of the life I had endured. My dreams, mirroring the old homestead, lay abandoned and weathered, yet they still linger, occupying a distant corner of my mind. Suddenly, I was drawn to a nearby sound of a lonesome whippoorwill, as though the bird was saying to me that he understood what I had been through.

My once brisk strides had transformed into gentle, deliberate movements, each step carrying the weight of accumulated years. This journey back home and down memory lane had proved to be a difficult one. Like so many times in the past, I sat there alone, understanding the need to proceed with caution. Trembling with a chill that resonated from the innermost depth of my soul, I stepped back onto the stage of the most treacherous years of my life. I did not like the person I had become. No longer was I the happy-go-lucky dreamer that bubbled over with expectations of a wonderful life, the one who saw good in everyone. Looking back through a different lens, I wondered why I even let him live. No one would have blamed me. The secrets and betrayals had been such a heavy weight to carry. But what choice did I have? None.

With the news received today, I was set free. After all these years, I felt I had a newfound hope. A hope I wondered so many times if I would live to see.

Two

Born Sandra Gail Phoenix, I lived on a seventy-two-acre farm that needed years of work. I was next to the oldest of four children. The only daughter of an ordinary, middle-class family. I valued the opinions of my family more than anything. Family always came first to me, no matter what.

Often, I climbed the hillside that led to the terrace above the old farmhouse overlooking a pure green valley of rolling acreage. For hours I would lie back on the plush green grass and detail exactly how I wanted my life to be in the future, a loving adored wife, a wonderful mother, and a nurse of expertise in my field.

The sky a bright blue and the wind blowing briskly through my long dark hair, I dreamed of making the crumbling farm into a replica of "Tara." I envisioned how happy Daddy would be to have a farm with working equipment to maintain the land and all the livestock. He loved cows, chickens, and horses. And I loved him. Oh, how my dream went on and on until something, a squirrel running up a nearby tree or the barking of my favorite dog, would retrieve me back to reality.

As I sprang to my feet smiling ear to ear, overflowing with energy, I found myself speaking out loud. "Someday, someday, I will make it happen just for my Daddy."

Daddy was a stocky, built man with calloused hands, certainly not a stranger to hard work. A man with a character of stone that everyone respected. A man of few words that had no trouble getting his point of view across, no matter the issue. No one dared to challenge him, his opinions displayed boldly in the look on his hardened face. Yet, I saw his gentleness, even as I watched him extinguish a camel cigarette by rolling it across the ashtray side to side. His complexity was refreshing. He adored his family — his wife, me, and the three boys.

He meant the world to me. There were no words to describe the admiration and love I had for Daddy. The feelings were mutual. I was his baby girl. Everyone called Daddy "Hud," but I called him Daddy because I wanted the whole world to know he was my Daddy. From an early age, I would say, "Daddy, I want to marry a man just like you."

"Why is that Baby Girl?"

"I want a man that will keep me safe like you do, Daddy, and will never leave me. When I marry, I will make sure it is forever."

No matter the circumstance, Daddy would always make everything okay. Day or night. He never let me down.

Daddy was off from work at the fire station. He worked twenty-four on and twenty-four off. He had showered, shaved, and dressed to go out.

"Hud, where are you going?" Mama called from the other room while she rocked the baby.

"I've got a show to play tonight, Virginia, don't you remember? I told you about it. I'll be coming in later." He shouted as he rushed out the door as if he were late.

Mama was often left at home with us children as Daddy went out and played his Gibson and sang. He stopped taking Mama with him because she would get jealous when women at the shows paid him attention. Then she would nag him about how he knew them, even if he did not. He said it was just easier for everyone if he just went by himself. He was not good at explaining this to Mama and her feelings would be hurt. Daddy was not at all perfect, but one thing was for sure: he loved his family.

I remember the lonely nights Mama would cry sitting home with four small children not knowing where he might be; was the show over or was he somewhere else? And then there were the many phone calls from other women claiming their rights to him. But through it all, Mama stood steadfast and faithful. She loved him with all her heart.

At the age of seven, I would stand by the picture window of the small two-bedroom house and pray for the 1960 blue Cadillac that he drove to appear. Sometimes thousands of tears would fall before that happened. I anxiously awaited his arrival, wondering what Mama's reaction would be. But I learned patience at an early age. Finally, his car would appear, and he would come in. I stood still behind the curtain so I could hear what was being said.

"Is that you, Hud?" Mama called from the kitchen.

"Yes, Hun, it's me."

"Why are you so late? Have you been drinking?"

"Here we go," he said under his breath as he went straight to the bedroom for the night.

Daddy does not know, but I remember all the nights he came home drinking and the fussing that went on between him and Mama. Many times, I would sleep on the floor outside their bedroom door for fear he would leave in the night, and I would not know it. Not that he had ever left before. He had not. But my best friend's dad had left his family, and

I couldn't imagine not having Daddy around. I loved him and Mama so much. They were my world. I would often sit in school wondering about home, if things were okay between them. I needed it to be. When I got home, I found out I had worried for no reason. Daddy and Mama would be talking and laughing and even hugging from time to time. This made me smile as I joined them for a hug.

Daddy would often get his Gibson out and sing while we all gathered around to listen. That is one of my best memories ever. It was all good until Daddy decided to go drinking with the guys. Mama was not at all one to argue a lot. I remember the night she gave Daddy the ultimatum.

"It's time you choose, Hud, either us or the drinking. You choose. If you don't stop the drinking, then I'll take the children and leave."

"Virginia, you know y'all are my world. I love you and the children. I promise, no more drinking. I promise. Just don't leave."

After that one time of Mama stating the facts, I never knew of Daddy drinking again. I guess he knew Mama was serious. Every morning that Daddy came home from work, I would rush to give him a good morning hug. I loved seeing him in his uniform, and he always smelled so good.

"I love you, Daddy."

"I love you too, Baby Girl."

"I love you too, Hud." Mama would smile coming from the kitchen, where she had breakfast waiting for him.

"I love you too, Hun." Then they kissed.

Daddy then hugged us both at the same time. This was the normal routine around our house, affection was often shown by all the family.

Daddy was a very handsome, rugged firefighter who stood six feet tall with big blue eyes and dark brown hair. I loved the fresh, clean scent of his aftershave and cologne that preceded him long before he entered a room and lingered long after he exited. I could often smell his Old Spice cologne just thinking about him. Not too much, not too little, just enough. He had an aura of charisma and women just seemed to flock to him. Even though, at times, he made decisions that I did not understand; I adored him, no matter what. There was no doubt at all that he loved and cherished his family. I often gave him the benefit of the doubt, wondering if it was just the women being aggressive and wanting to cause trouble. There was never any real proof that the accusations were true. So, in my eyes, I was his Baby Girl, and I loved him with all my heart. I always had and always would.

Mama was a waitress and had always worked hard to help support the family. She was frail, modest, unpretentious, and always busy striving to please her man and take care of her children. She was an example of the perfect mama that fulfilled all expectations of the role of a wife and a mother. Despite the trials and tribulations of Daddy's so-called flings and the financial struggles, Mama prayed hard, and God answered keeping the family together with love and forgiveness. It was like she had a supernatural strength when it came to her man and her children. Nothing nor anyone would take her man or her children from her. She was nonconfrontational. She fought her battles on her knees and God took care of it, whatever it was at the time.

In early 1970 Mama went to work at the cotton mill because the restaurant where she worked was closing. The mill was just across the street from the restaurant and the mill bosses often dined there at lunch. Mama's personality was one of a humble serving nature, always smiling and greeting people at the diner with a sincere, caring disposition. The mill bosses delighted in her serving them. After hearing about the closing of the diner, one of the bosses offered Mama a job. She accepted.

Mama and I were very close. As a matter of fact, I wished I was more like her. Mama was so kind, filled with love for everyone and so forgiving. She believed in Jesus, and she lived her life in such a way that his love was shown through her life daily. She deposited value into everyone she met.

I would often listen to Mama as she always prayed for her family. I believed that when Mama prayed, even the angels stood still and listened. It was as if Mama thought of nothing else but Jesus, her man, and her children. They were what mattered most to her. She was the epitome of what a mother's love should be.

Three

With graduation nearing, I knew I'd need a job to help support myself while pursuing my college education to become a nurse.

"Good morning, Sandra, you are here very early," Ms. Jones commented.

"Yes, ma'am, I am searching for a financial aid program to help me with my tuition for nursing school. Times are often financially difficult around the farm. It will be hard on my family to help me fulfill my dream. I don't want to be a burden on them."

As Mrs. Jones listened intently, she sat with the sweetest smile on her face. She and I had grown close over the past three years, as I would come and help her in the library every chance I had. I loved learning from her. She was a very distinguished, caring person. Only a few days later, Mrs. Jones came up to me while I was shelving books.

"Sandra, I have some good news to share with you. I spoke to a friend of mine, and he has agreed to help fund your college tuition and not only that, but to award you with a full scholarship."

I could hardly believe what I was hearing.

"For real, Mrs. Jones?" I rushed to give her a hug with tears of joy.

"For real, Sandra. Come and I will introduce you two, and together you can work out the details."

"How will I ever thank you, Mrs. Jones?"

"You can thank me by being the best nurse you can be. And I know you will be just that."

Only a few weeks after graduation, I decided to seek employment to help support myself through college. How blessed I was to get the full scholarship, but I knew I would need gas money and other things. Two weeks later, there was an opening in the cloth room at the Mill where Mama worked. I was the lucky girl. I would start within the week. I was so excited to get this job. I would now be able to continue my college classes for my nursing career and work, too.

Little did I know this would be the place that I would meet someone that would change my life forever. This is where it all began… It was only the beginning of eight years of destitution, terror, suffering, heartache, pain, and torment, all wrapped up in misery. Would I survive?

Four

I was only seventeen the first time I laid eyes on him. Working in an ancient cotton mill in the low section of town while attending college to pursue my nursing dream. One of my three dreams since early childhood.

A tall figuration shadowed on the sidewalk as the moonlight shone down upon him. He swayed with perfect balance, like an oak tree in the wind. With each step, he moved with a confident, fluent movement. It was the second shift of mill workers racing to their cars after the mill whistle blew, releasing them from their long, toil-driven eight hours of mill work. I watched until he was out of sight.

The next evening, as I entered the mill door, I saw Ms. Emm.

"Hey, Ms. Emm!" I ran to catch up with her, then stopped and gasped for a breath of air.

"Hello, Sandra. You seem to be in a hurry today."

"I wanted to ask you a question, if you don't mind."

"Sure, what is it, Love?"

"You know all the cute guys that work around here. I noticed a tall handsome guy that sometimes leaves when we do. He comes down from the upstairs cloth room as we are leaving at night." I paused to take in a deep breath. "Do you know anything about him?"

"Of course, I do. He has worked in the upstairs in the cloth room for maybe a year, seems to be a nice guy. But he is very quiet and stays to himself."

"Thanks, Ms. Emm. I'll talk to you later."

Only on occasion did I get a glimpse of him. But when I did, there was a longing to be with him that burned deep within. My blood ran hot with just a glimpse of him in passing. This was not at all like me. My character was impeccable with old fashion beliefs, especially where men were concerned. But now, there I stood in the distance, wondering what it would be like if he noticed me. Then I would watch him drive away and my imagination would run freely, as I hoped for just one more glimpse of him on another day.

All my girlfriends from school had guys that they had been dating for a couple of years or more and there I stood looking for my prince charming. Then I saw him, I thought, *wow he looks just like what a prince charming should look like.* I had never been drawn to someone whom I had never met before. But now I was.

"Hey girl, what are you gazing at?" Iris's voice jolted me back to reality.

Iris had become one of my very best friends since I began working at the mill. She had a petite frame, short legs and was stocky built with an incredible personality. Shy was never a word in her vocabulary, especially around all the cute guys that worked at the mill. She did seem to be a bit jealous of my legs, as she would make a lot of jokes about them. After all, they were one of the two traits that distinguished me. They were legs that should be insured, if you know what I mean. At least I had been told that on occasion.

"Oh, just daydreaming," I barely whispered.

"Why don't you just let him know that you'd like to go out with him?"

"I could never do that."

Then I walked away with a vision of Grandmama in the shadows, smiling and so proud. Iris followed as I sat down at the break table. She joined me.

"Why are you so hesitant to let him know you like him," she asked.

"I am not at all aggressive with men. I was taught to believe a woman should never ask a man out. This was a belief passed to me from Grandmama."

"Don't you think that's a little old fashion?"

"No, Grandmama is a lady of great wisdom and honor. She is always there when I need her. And she is invariably on track with her advice."

Grandmama seemed to have an insight into things that I wondered how she ever knew about. Once I was troubled about a situation and had not shared that with anyone. She came to me and said, "You know you need to trust your gut, Sandra, and it will all work out. Never let anyone, especially an older man, take advantage of you. Never be afraid to tell me anything." Then she gave me a big hug and walked away. How did she know I wondered?

But I took her advice and worked it out. She has consistently been available when I was in need of anything. I share my innermost thoughts and desires with her. Things that I could never tell anyone else, I can trust her with. We often spent all day fishing, talking, and being together. I take to heart everything she has to offer.

"Wow, she sounds incredible."

"She is a distinguished, intelligent, and beautiful woman. Standing five foot eight inches tall, she is of Cherokee descent. Her features are those of a respected older woman of a native tribe portrayed in an old movie. Perhaps it was from her ancestry that she has such insight into unknown things. Nevertheless, she is the smartest woman I have ever known. My love for her is unconditional and I hunger for her approval in all that I do. My admiration for her exceeds indescribable."

"I never knew my grandmama like that. We lived in different towns. Sounds like I missed out," Iris shared.

"I will introduce you to her soon. I know you will love her, and she will certainly love you."

"I can't wait to meet her."

The following weekend Iris and I were off from the mill, so I invited her down to the farm to meet the rest of my family. She had already met Mama working at the mill.

"Your mama reminds me of my own mom back in Tennessee," Iris said. "They are both petite and always have a smile on their face."

Iris connected very quickly with Grandmama and in return Grandmama grew fond of her as time passed. She loved that she was always smiling and joking around with such a jolly disposition. Grandmama related in that she too liked to joke around and laugh. But not only did Iris quickly become like part of our family, she really connected with my older brother, Jake. They began dating shortly after this visit to the farm.

Five

I was just coming in from helping in the field with the garden. Everyone in the family, including Grandmama participated in the chores around the farm. There was a phone call for me.

"It's the tall, dark, handsome young man from the mill," Mama announced.

"You are kidding, right?"

"See for yourself." She handed the phone to me with a huge smile.

I had waited for this call for some time. I was not very experienced at dating simply because not many guys have asked to be honest. Being elated and at the same time petrified, fearful of saying the wrong thing, I drew a deep breath as I looked at the receiver in my hand, trembling with excitement.

"Hello," I said, trying not to convey my overexcited emotion.

The deep, manly voice on the other end took my breath away. "Hello there, this is Charles Black from the mill."

From that moment, I was in a daze. Not sure just what was said, but I think it was a typical conversation of small talk and then an invitation to the movies. Of course, I accepted. As I hung up the phone, I was overcome with chills of excitement that ran from the top of my head down my spine to my toes. I was in a state of disbelief that this had finally happened. The tall, dark, handsome mill worker had asked me out. I had mastered the phone call that I thought was a dream come true. I never in my wildest imagination could have anticipated the illusion that would unfold in the time to come. With only a couple of days until it would happen, I could hardly contain myself.

"Oh, Mama, can you believe it? He called and asked me out. I had no idea that he had even noticed me working at the mill. How do you think he got my number?"

Mama was delighted that I was so thrilled. I was ecstatic and went on and on. Mama just smiled and shook her head.

"I don't even know how to act on a date," I giggled at just the thought.

"Oh, sweetheart, you'll do just fine. Just be yourself."

"I must call Iris and tell her."

"Hello."

"Hey, it's me. Iris, you won't believe who called and asked me out today." Before she had a chance to answer, I blurted out, "Charles Black! Can you believe it?"

"How did he get your number?"

"I have no idea. Iris, you didn't—"

"No, it wasn't me, I promise."

"Iris, I know you've dated a lot, but I haven't, and I'm really nervous."

"Oh, girl, you'll do fine. Just be yourself. Everyone loves you, Sandra.",

"Thanks, but I hope I don't mess this up. Got to run now. Talk to you later."

"We will talk another day."

Two days later, he drove up in a shiny dark blue car that looked long enough to be a limo. But that was just my excited state, it was really a Buick

Impala. He rang the doorbell. As I opened the door, there he stood—tall, dark and neatly dressed, wearing an intriguing smile.

"Come in and meet my parents," I said.

"Hello ma'am," he said, nodding his head.

"Nice to meet you, Charles," Daddy greeted him.

"Sir." He reached to shake Daddy's hand.

"Young man."

He politely met my parents with remarkable manners. I was completely captured. It was just as I knew it would be, for the moment anyway.

"Well, shall we go?" Charles said, as he guided me to the door with his hand on the small of my back.

"Bye, love y'all."

"Don't be late," Daddy added.

"Yes, sir," Charles said in a military tone.

Charles Black seemed confident, yet guarded. He opened my car door for me. This was the first time anyone had opened my car door. I can't explain how that made me feel. I was a nervous wreck, not being able to erase the smile from my face. Still in a state of shock that this was really happening. As I sat down in the seat looking up at him, He stood staring down into my eyes as if to search my soul for any hidden secrets. I could feel my face blushing. I had never seen eyes so dark. His hair was neatly shaped with a swag loosely swept to the side. He had an overall intimidating presence, in a good way. A way that made my curiosity rise. After a few moments, never speaking a word, He smiled and shut my door.

As he drove down the long driveway, Charles had nothing to say. Occasionally, he would glance over at me without saying anything. Was he sizing me up? What was he thinking? Trying to break the ice, so to speak, in my excited state, I asked, "How did you get my telephone number?"

Slow with his answer, he replied. "I asked your mom's friend, Shirley, and she gave it to me. Which movie would you like to see?"

"It doesn't matter to me," I said. "Have you worked at the mill very long?"

"No."

It was obvious he did not want to talk about the mill. I glanced over at him, out of the corner of my eye from time to time, unable to stop fidgeting while trying to carry on a conversation that seemed to be twenty questions with short answers. There was an air of mystery that surrounded him, followed by a long period of silence. I was so relieved when we entered the movie parking lot. Charles got out and went around to open my door. I was mesmerized as he extended his hand as I exited the car. Not really sure why. I wasn't even sure how to act on a first date. I had never been on a real date like this before. So, I remained very reserved.

Charles was very arrogant in his approach. He had little to nothing to say. Maybe he thought I wasn't intelligent enough to carry on a conversation with him. What did we have in common? A country girl meets a tall, dark, handsome stranger. Why did he choose me?

After the movie, Charles once again opened my car door without saying a word. He entered the car, cranked it and headed in the direction to take me home. Still not a word.

"I really liked the movie. How about you?"

"It was okay."

He was not at all interested in talking about the movie. Suddenly, my stomach growled really loud. I was so hungry. I thought we would probably go somewhere to eat after the movie, so I had not eaten earlier. He did not acknowledge he had even heard it. Out of embarrassment, I remained quiet. Would he ever ask me out again? When we arrived at my house, I invited him in.

"No, I need to be going." He walked me to the door and kissed me on the cheek.

"I'll talk to you later."

As I stood and watched him drive down the long dirt driveway, the excitement of this date was entangled with intimidation and a superior attitude radiating from him. I would come to realize that I was not mistaken about the mysterious aura encompassing this tall, dark, handsome young man. Was this feeling a warning? A warning that I so easily dismissed. It would be later, much too late, when I'd find out the truth.

Six

"**G**ood morning, sweetheart. Well, how was your date last night?" Mama asked as she poured our morning coffee.

"It was just so..." searching through the myriad of adjectives I wished I could use to answer Mama, awkward was all I could come up with.

"Maybe he has not been on many dates either," Mama suggested.

"I have no idea why I am so drawn to this guy. What is so intriguing about him that makes me think of him all the time. He certainly is not Mr. Personality. Mama, I know I don't really know that much about dating, but it just wasn't quite what I had imagined. I was so uncomfortable."

"Sweetheart, you know you don't have to go out with him again. Just say you are busy."

There were other guys at the mill that paid me a little attention, but no one had asked me out. There was definitely not an attraction to any of them the way there was to Charles. What was it about him?

He waited a couple of days before he phoned. It seemed he was easier to talk to over the phone. However, he was very evasive about discussing anything about himself or his family. I, with my charismatic personality, could usually get anyone to talk. This was the other trait that distinguished me, a charismatic personality that was contagious, bubbling over and lavishly spilling onto others like a peaceful, slow-flowing mountain stream. But not with Charles Black; he was very standoffish and disinterested in what I had to say. His conversations were of no substance. Until he shared that he knew a lot about me—where my dad worked, that I was pursuing a nursing career, my favorite color was red, small tidbits of personal information that were private. He would not reveal his source.

At first, I thought his inquiry meant he really liked me. But then I wasn't sure. I had a very uncomfortable feeling, a feeling of being violated.

It took several dates before I felt at ease with Charles. Often, I wondered why I'd even agreed to go. But as one date led to another—usually going to the movies, out for pizza, hanging around the farm, riding the motorcycle, just easy simple things—six months had passed very quickly.

I should have known something wasn't exactly right when he was so vague about his family. He was not at all willing to let me meet them, nor did he want to talk about them. I could see in the far distance where he lived when en route from the mill to my house. It was, from what I could see, a very nice house that sat secluded on a hill.

The mystery of the hidden family on the hill bothered me, but not enough to doubt the tall, dark, handsome man of my dreams—Charles Black.

No one at the mill could shed any light on the mysterious invisible family that was nestled in the far distance. It seemed that Charles shared nothing and was quite a loner. I often wondered if he even had a family. What was the big secret?

There was nothing in the world that meant more to me than family, my Daddy, my Mama, and three brothers. And even though things were rocky in my younger days with Daddy's so-called flings and drinking, things were great now. After having weathered the stormy trials, they seemed to have brought our family even closer together. I contributed that to a mama who stood steadfast in her faith and prayed every day. God had answered a lot of Mama's prayers and the family was better for it.

As time went on, I learned very little about the man of my dream's mysterious family, his childhood, or even his present life. However, working at the ancient mill, rumors often rumbled the halls like ghosts of the past revealing themselves.

I had gone outside looking for Iris on my break, and as I was returning to my department, I noticed two rough looking guys from the finishing department gathered smoking at the side of the building. Just as I approached, I overheard Charles' name. It caught my attention. I stopped dead in my tracks and remained in the shadow, out of their sight. They were discussing how Charles had narked on a group of guys.

"Seems Mr. Black thinks he is very intelligent and an expert at scheming."

"Does he know they know about his deal in exchange for information to be placed on a job with a local power company that would originally take years to get?"

"We are to get rid of him before he becomes aware."

My heart was racing as fear mounted inside me. What had I gotten myself into? I knew I did not want these guys to know that I had overheard their conversation. They might want to get rid of me, too. I stayed hidden until they put their cigarettes out and went back inside. I was so scared; I backed up and went a different way to my department. I wanted to make sure no one saw me. As I made my way to my worktable, I hoped no one would see how shaken I was. I'm sure I looked pale and clammy. I could hardly concentrate on my work until my shift ended. Baffled with fright at what this could mean, I pondered over and over what I had heard, desperately waiting for Charles to phone. Was this some big drug ring or even the Mafia? Had Charles placed himself, as well as me, in a position that we could be killed? The two guys from the finishing department were very vague in their description of what getting rid of him entailed. I paced the floor nervously, spilling the cup of coffee I had just made. I could not concentrate on anything else waiting anxiously to talk to Charles.

I was still waiting for his call that same night. Never having phoned Charles for fear that his mother, if he truly had one, might answer. And what would Grandmama think? After all, a woman just did not call a man. The call came two hours later than it normally did.

"Hi, Baby, what's going on?" His voice had no worry at all.

"I need some answers, Charles. I am so scared," my voice trembled.

"What's this about?" he laughed.

"Maybe a drug ring?" I whispered.

"Look, just calm down and I'll be right over."

There was a click, then a dial tone. He was gone. It was obvious that Charles did not want to discuss this over the phone. I took a step back and swallowed hard, then hung up the phone. He arrived in less than fifteen minutes. As I opened the door, He could see the troubled look in my eyes. I did not understand how he could look so calm, cool and collected.

"Hey, Baby. Want to tell me what's going on now?" he asked, as he took me by the hand to walk with him.

I willingly stepped out on the porch, and we walked arm in arm to the field down by the decrepit barn far away from the house, so no one could overhear our conversation. I expressed my fears and explained what I had overheard at the mill earlier that day. He was very inquisitive of who these guys were.

"I have no idea who they are," I shared, becoming more apprehensive. "I just happened upon them. They never saw me."

Charles had a very inappropriate grin and laugh. He seemed to laugh at me as the tears of fear overflowed down my cheeks.

"This is all just a mistake, a misunderstanding, nothing for you to worry about, Sandra." He spoke in a very authoritative manner.

"You are never to mention this again to me or anyone else. Do you understand?" He spoke adamantly with that inappropriate smile still on his face. Then he reached and wiped a tear from my cheek and said, "It's all okay, I promise."

His touch, at times, could be gentle but then mixed with a controlling voice, making me feel safe and scared all at the same time. He would display signs of a strong, loving, protective man, then suddenly switch to a very controlling and in charge demeanor.

Seven

It was only the following week that Charles called with the news that he would be starting a new job with the local power company. This news rekindled the original fear inside of me all over again. I sat remembering and meditating on the conversation I had overheard only a week ago.

Had he been rewarded with a new job in return for his narking? What was he really into? Was I just overreacting? I hated these swells of reasoning that seem to appear out of nowhere.

He was gentle at times, charming even, then so inconsiderate at other times. I convinced myself that it was all just coincidental circumstances and quickly dismissed the awful frightening thoughts, as I felt guilty thinking such thoughts of Charles.

I had to admit I found the mystery of him a little compelling. However, I was totally oblivious to the web that was being weaved around me. Nevertheless, the relationship continued. As the days went by, I fell more and more for the tall, dark, handsome man. Yet in so many ways he remained a stranger to me.

I still had not been allowed to meet his family. He refused to discuss anything about who he really was or where he came from. Until one day,

Charles and I were riding his motorcycle in a deserted area of nothing but dirt roads that ran on for what seemed like forever. As we rode, the wind was blowing; the smells of the summer day surrounded us. Overhead, the birds were flying and singing, the wildflowers covered the hillsides in a splendor array of colors. I was so infatuated with this mystery man of mine—smitten and in a fantasy world all my own. It was wonderful. As I snuggled as close to him as I could, holding on tightly, my imagination running free and wild, I felt like all my dreams were within my reach. It was times like this that I felt we were meant to be.

Suddenly, as we rounded a curve on one of the back dirt roads, I was jolted back to reality as we came upon an accident. A man with a small child had been thrown from their motorcycle. Lying on the ground was a man convulsing and blood oozing from his nose and ears. I immediately rushed to the child and quickly assessed that he was not severely injured. While at the same time, assessing the man from a distance to make sure he was breathing. I could see that he was and that he had an open airway. It was best not to move him until the paramedics got there for fear of causing more damage or losing his open airway. Charles could see the urgency.

"I'm going for help," he said, and immediately hopped back on his motorcycle and sped off.

I remained at the scene with the child and man while Charles rode away. I wondered just how long it would take him and where he would go to call for help. I comforted the child as I paced and prayed. The man was unresponsive and continued to convulse.

"Everything is going to be okay, Baby Boy," I said.

Immediately, there were several people gathered around the scene and then Charles returned. Having heard the call for help over the police scanners, people came from close by. I instructed them it was best to wait for the ambulance to arrive before moving the man as long as he was breathing.

I stood close by him to continually assess him and his breathing just in case he needed assistance. Of course, with my nurses training, I was certified in CPR. I continued to hold the child and comfort him.

The ambulance arrived soon after Charles had gotten back. They quickly assessed the man, placed him and the child on the stretcher and took them away. The excitement had ended, and the crowd disbursed. There remained only one tall, dark-headed woman standing and staring at me.

She slowly approached me and asked, "Charles, are you going to introduce her?"

He made a cunning remark under his breath that only I could hear.

"No, I'm not," he said in a harsh, degrading tone.

He and I were astraddle his motorcycle, and he suddenly sped away leaving the woman just standing there. She wore the all-familiar inappropriate smile that I had seen so many times on Charles' face. I had such a disturbed sense of emotion. Not able to comprehend what had just happened. Who was this woman? Why would, and how could, Charles be so rude, so disrespectful to another human being. He was almost barbaric in his response to this dark-headed stranger with a familiar inappropriate smile.

He then went in the direction of the mysterious house on the distant hill, where the mysterious family lived. He needed to clean himself up after helping with the accident. In a state of confusion, I entered the mystery house that sat secluded far upon the hill. A gut feeling made me hesitant about stepping inside as though something inside would harm me. Maybe this was another warning?

It was a medium-sized home, neat and clean. It was dark and cold. No family portraits to view on the walls. The furniture was big and heavy antiques. The ancient smells that come with antiques were evident. There was a heaviness felt immediately as I stepped inside. As if there were secrets that were hiding, and strangers were not welcome.

Charles led me straight down the hall allowing me to wash my hands, then to his bedroom. It was a small room with guns hanging all over the walls. It was not a peaceful domain. Just a nightstand and a twin-size bed. A bed much too small for such a tall young man. He quickly took a change of clothes to the bathroom instructing me to remain in his room while he changed. So uncomfortable with his demand, I did not move an inch. He was gone for what seemed like forever to me. Upon his return, he closed his bedroom door and locked it. I had become even more uncomfortable at that point. I sat on the very edge of the bed, meanwhile he stretched out across the bed. Having never been in a boy's bedroom before, I wasn't sure I wanted to be there now. I noticed a phone on the nightstand and asked permission to phone my Mama. I knew my parents would be worried because we had left on the motorcycle hours before.

"Hi, Mama, just thought I'd check in, didn't want you to worry. We happened upon an accident involving a man and little boy. Time got away as we helped them. I'll tell you all about it when I get home shortly. Love you."

"Ok, Baby Girl, be careful, see you soon. Love you too," Mama replied lovingly.

Just as I hung up the phone, there was a loud, resounding knock on the door of Charles' bedroom. A knock so hard that it could have taken the door off the hinges. I jumped to my feet as I gasped. What in the world? I was frozen in time. A very loud, angry voice screamed from the other side of the door.

"Open this door, Charles! This is my house, and you are not going to do this in my house," Charles' mother shouted in outrage.

I could feel my heart beating in my throat. My stomach plummeted as though I had just been released down the tallest roller coaster in the world, then came the nausea. I shook all over, paralyzed with fear. Charles jumped up, cursing the voice behind the locked door.

"Come on, we are getting the hell out of here," he yelled at me.

He opened the door, grabbed my hand pulling me with him as he pushed by the tall, dark-headed woman that was at the scene of the accident just a little while before. Now she was irate.

"How dare you bring that girl in my house."

"Shut up, I live here too, Bitch."

"Go to hell."

With all the screaming and threatening each other, I thought I was going to throw up. I had never encountered anything like this before. Even though things were rocky in my younger days with my Daddy's drinking and so-called flings, never once did I encounter anyone in my family screaming, cussing or acting like this. Not ever.

This was my introduction to Charles' mom. As we exited, his mother was still screaming at Charles.

"I am going to call her mother and tell her what she has done. How horrible and despicable her daughter's behavior has been today. She has disrespected me and my house," Charles' mother continued threatening.

She was so enraged that she looked as though fire was coming from her eyes. I had never witnessed such absurd behavior coming from two adults. I had done nothing but use the phone, but I felt appalled, confused and injured as if a bomb had ignited and the shrapnel had definitely hit me.

What would my folks do, if indeed, this unrestrained woman phoned them with such a story? Even though my family was not perfect, I had never experienced such an explosive exchange of obscenities between a mother and a son. My three brothers were so loving and respectful of my parents: especially our Mama. They were very protective of Mama and of me. On any occasion or circumstance, I was taught to show love and respect, especially for my parents. They, in return, showed respect to us children. Never in my greatest imagination would I have thought of talking that way to my parents and certainly not cussing them, that was unheard of in my house. I had never encountered such a family, but then Charles and his mother didn't fit the definition of family.

This was just unbelievable. I could hardly accept that I had been a witness to a mother telling her son to "go to hell." It was like a horror movie. This was her son, her own flesh and blood. This was his mother that brought him into this world. Call me naive if you like, but I could not comprehend that a world like this really existed. Love was our family's foundation and there was no evidence of that here. Was this the way of life at the mysterious hidden house with the mystery family? What else did they have to hide?

Charles pulled off the road onto a dirt road to try and calm me down. He slipped his arm around my shoulder and pulled me close to him. The tears were coming so hard and fast I was sobbing uncontrollably. As the pit of my stomach was churning, I fought the urge to hurl. I had never in my life been made to feel so cheap and so dirty. I had truly not done anything wrong. How would I ever face this woman again?

"I never want to see that woman again, ever!" I said frankly.

"She is just an evil bitch that wants to control and embarrass me. I don't even know who she is most of the time."

He was still so enraged with his mother. He continued to speak of her as if she was someone he despised.

"You will never have to see her again. I promise you. It will be okay," Charles repeated over and over. "It will be okay."

I pulled myself together after a little while.

"Please, just take me home."

Nothing more was said. He let me out and left. I was relieved as I entered my home to find everything peaceful. Daddy was intently watching TV, smoking his camel cigarette and Mama was sitting on the sofa reading her Bible. It was obvious as I was greeted by their smiles that the uncontrollable, irate dark-haired woman had not phoned. I excused myself to my room for the night. I wanted so much to discuss what had occurred at Charles' with my parents, but I felt it was so abnormal that they would forbid me to ever see Charles again or to go there again. Not that I had any plans of ever returning there, not ever. My Mama had picked up on the fact that I seemed upset when I came in. My face appeared pale, and she could tell I had been crying. She gave me a few minutes before knocking on my bedroom door to tell me good night with a kiss as she always does.

"I'm here if you need to talk, whenever you're ready. Love you, Baby Girl," Mama said with a loving voice.

Charles phoned the next night as though nothing had happened.

"What's up, Baby," he said nonchalantly.

It was obvious that this was another topic that he had no intention of ever discussing again. As I pondered back over what had happened, I wondered how his mother would know how to contact my parents. She had never met me. She did not even know my name, according to Charles. Supposedly, he did not share information with his mother. Or did he?

I was more drawn to him now than ever. He must have felt so unloved. How could a mother treat her own child like his mother had treated him. I felt an indescribable sadness for him that I could not define. Overwhelmed, I felt that I needed to help make this right for him. Unable to shake this feeling of a helpless child being abused with no one to love him all these years, was haunting. I could not fathom what that would be like as a child or an adult. Having so many unanswered questions, this just seemed to justify all the excuses I was trying to knit together to explain Charles' weird unacceptable behavior and to calm some of my mixed emotions.

About a week later, after the motorcycle accident, I received a telephone call from a local detective.

"Hello, Ms. Pheonix, this is detective Richards with the local police department. I would like to ask you a few questions about the man from the motorcycle accident last week."

"Of course," I said.

"Had you ever seen that man before?"

"No sir."

"You don't know his name?"

"No sir, we were riding by ourselves, my boyfriend and I. We just came upon him. We didn't see him wreck. He was already lying on the ground."

"What is your boyfriend's name?"

"Charles Black."

"Have you ever seen Mr. Black with the man in the accident?"

"No sir. May I ask what this is all about?"

"The man on the motorcycle is Mr. Bolero. He is not someone you would want to mingle with. We have been investigating him for a while. He is not a nice man. You might want to share with Mr. Black to keep his distance from Mr. Bolero."

As I hung up the phone, I could not quite comprehend what this was about. It appears as though the detective was trying to get a message to Charles behind the scenes. If they had been watching this man, then he knew I did not know him. Or was he trying to inform me that Charles was not someone I should trust. I debated whether I should share this information with him or not. I decided not to talk about this over the phone, because I wanted to look into his eyes to retrieve his reaction to this call. On his next visit, I briefly shared some of the information with him.

"What was the detective's name?"

"Detective Richards, I think."

"I'm not worried about Richards," he said with the inappropriate smile across his face. It was as though he was very familiar with the detective. But why? This was never mentioned again. But it remained filed in my memory.

Eight

Several months had passed as Charles continued to call on me. As we were together more, the invite came. His mother had sent an invitation for me to join their family for dinner.

"After all, if her son was going to spend so much time with this girl, she felt she should get to know her," the invite read.

I was more than very reluctant. I vividly remembered my first introduction to Charles' mother. I was not impressed to say the least. And I for sure did not want to go there. But he had become so controlling and insisted that I accept the invite. He had promised I would never have to face this woman again. But this is just one of many, many broken promises to come. It was a beautiful clear night. The stars were just breaking through to fill the sky with a twinkling tapestry. The wind slightly whispering through the trees and the crickets and frogs in unison could be heard in the distance. As Charles drove up the long dirt road to the mystery house on the hill, I sat in silence. My stomach became knotted, a pain that took my breath away as if I were being led before a judge, jury and then a firing squad. The uncertainty overwhelmed me; trembling on the inside as if I were in the arctic without the proper attire. There was a gloomy feeling that surrounded me of an impending doom. I felt as if I was entering an area of very dangerous explosives. The fear of the unknown engulfed me. I should have known that this was not a good beginning to a happy ending. Deep in thought and unaware of my surroundings, I jumped and gasped for a breath as he opened the car door. We were there at the mystery house on the hill.

The door opened. There stood the dark-headed woman with the all-familiar smile on her face. I had not gotten a good look at her at our first meeting. She was a very attractive woman, standing about five feet nine inches tall. Her hair was jet black and lay in big soft curls on her shoulders. She was well dressed in slacks and a collared shirt.

"Come on in," Mrs. Black excitedly expressed.

Mrs. Black acted as if this was our first meeting. She was very boisterous and in control, instructing everyone where their places were at the table. She never stopped smiling that inappropriate grin the entire time we were there. As though she had a well-hidden secret that she would use if she needed to. Exhibiting a dominating persona as that of a queen with authority. The meal was already prepared as Charles and I entered, and everyone immediately took their places at the table as instructed. Charles' dad, a very docile, laid back, quaint man, sat at one end of the table. He was not as tall as Charles' mother. He was a short and stocky built man with a shy grin. He wore large rimmed black glasses and had little to nothing to say. He was very submissive and only spoke when spoken to.

"Hello" was the only word he spoke.

At the head of the table was the ruler, the Queen herself, Charles' mother. It would not have taken anyone long to figure out who was the head of this domain. Across the table was Charles' brother, Brody. He was probably the happiest of the bunch. He seemed to be the pick of the litter, so to speak. He was about the same height as his dad and wore his hair long and feathered to the side. He wore black rimmed glasses, just as his dad did. He was a talker and the whole family listened intensely. He covered many subjects as he rambled on and on. However, I blocked it all out, just wishing for the time to pass quickly. Across the table sitting next to Brody was Charles' younger brother, Mitch. He had light colored hair with big blue eyes, and to be honest, he favored no one gathered at the table. He remained quiet throughout the entire meal. Only a simple, "Hello," upon our arrival was heard from him all evening. Charles had nothing to contribute to the conversation at all. It was more than obvious that these three siblings had nothing in common. It appeared they did not even like each other. I sat in amazement. How could this group of people consider themselves a family?

The table was elegant with fine crystal and china. My family did not even own a set of china, but I am sure that Mrs. Black had investigated me enough to know that we were just simple country folks and china would not be present on our country table. Seemed this was the way that the Queen liked to communicate. Through the route of intimation and the degrading of others.

For the first time in my life, I was served something that was green and bushy on top. Having no idea how or what part of it I was supposed to eat or even if I was supposed to eat it, I watched to see if the others ate it and what parts they ate, then followed suit.

"Do you not like broccoli, Sandra?" Mrs. Black asked arrogantly.

"Yes, ma'am." I lied. How would I know? I'd never had it before. Being a bundle of nerves, I really did not even want anything to eat. And on top of that she was watching every move I made. An intimidation strategy. As a country girl. I did not care for this staged spectacle. Charles' mother had wasted her undertaking to either intimidate or control me. Even though I had been sheltered all my life, I was not without common sense. I refused to be intimidated again by this woman. I would stand my ground. I had intuition of evil when evil was present. No mention of the first encounter between Mrs. Black and me at the mystery house was ever brought to light. However, Charles' mother with a raised deep brown eyebrow spoke out of a dead silence.

"Sandra, my father worked with your dad as a fire fighter."

She just sat with a condescending smile staring directly into my big blue eyes.

Feeling very uneasy as she glared at me, I took this as a warning and remained silent. Just in the way that she presented it with a malicious inappropriate smile that spread across her face, I knew to be aware. And aware I was of the evil that radiated from this giant of a woman. The Queen of this mystery abode made her presence overwhelming, hovering over all that entered. The meal was finally concluded, and Charles quickly excused us.

"We must be going. We have a date at the movies, and we will barely make it now."

"Thank you so much for the dinner. I enjoyed it very much. It was nice meeting you all." I graciously stated in one long breath as we exited to the car.

I was so relieved once inside the car and the door was shut. Only silence could be heard as we rode to the movie theater. To me, the mystery house was becoming increasingly like a haunted evil house with stories. If only the walls could talk. The volcanic impending doom lingered in my gut for the rest of the evening. What had I gotten myself into? The atmosphere around the table and in the mystery house certainly did not resemble any characteristics of family that I was used to. There was no love, no affection, and no respect. A feeling of immoral, deceitful, cruel and malicious air was suspended over all of them. A place where only bad and evil reigned; and the greatest of the evil was Charles' mother—the Queen.

As time speedily raced by, Charles' and my relationship became more involved. A year had passed, and I was caught up in a web that had been spun tightly around me. He had become very demanding, obsessive and manipulative. He would show up at my house unannounced and expected me to always be there waiting.

"I can find plenty of other girls that would be more than willing to wait for me," he adamantly threatened. "If you are going somewhere, you are to ask me."

He was a master at deceiving, and he loved playing mind games. He had not been this way at the beginning. Or had he? Had I been blind to it? In a moment of heated anger stemming from my failure to ask his permission to leave my house, he scolded me.

"I am connected to some very resourceful associates. I work with them in stealing cars and disposing of them for people who want to collect insurance." He was bragging and sending a message of warning to me. "I can get away with anything and not get caught. So, if you ever think of crossing me, you'd better think twice. Just so you know." The inappropriate grin plastered across his face.

After learning of lies, deceit, and criminal acts that he had been involved in, I knew it was too late for me to get out. I knew too much. I kept quiet as overwhelming fear and anxiety overtook me, too afraid even to speak. At this point, I knew there was no one I could tell, not even Grandmama, for her own safety. There was no place I could hide. I was now bound by this man, a total stranger. How could I have thought that I was desperately in love? During this time, Charles had been transferred to a position in South Georgia, through the local power company. He had not even really discussed the transfer with me except to say he was going the upcoming weekend and that it would mean more money for our future. He would only be able to come home on weekends, every other weekend.

"I'll be able to send money home for you to put in an account for the future," he said. He was a real expert manipulator, and he really knew how to work me.

"What account?"

He then instructed me, "You are to open an account at the bank for the future. I will send money home to you and you can also contribute money to the account."

We were not even engaged. He had never even mentioned marriage. But he seemed to think he owned me, as though he had taken me captive. There had never been any exchange of affectionate words such as I love you or I can't wait to be with you forever. He was certainly not a passionate, doting person. He was kinder and a little caring at the beginning but now, he showed no emotion, just a big inappropriate grin that seemed to be inherited from the Queen.

Nine

Christmas was just around the corner. Charles had been at his new position in South Georgia for several months now. He visited with me on the weekends that he was able to make it home. I would wait sometimes for hours by the phone when he was away. He might call or he might not. I was always so excited when he did. Being upset about all the hours I waited frivolously just faded with the sound of his voice. I was convinced that the criminal involvement that Charles had been a part of was his past and he no longer needed to associate with that type of activity now that he had a good job. I had a knack for dismissing the abnormal behavior that Charles exhibited, rationalizing it in my mind that he had been abused and needed someone to love him. He never mentioned having any friends from school or friends he grew up with. No close cousins to mention. He seemed to have no one that he was close to. So, of course, I thought that I had to fulfill that role for him.

I often fantasized about what it would be like when the lover of my dreams did propose to me. A good-looking man with a gentle smile and a gleam in his eye; a man that would touch me with a stroke that was so warm and tender; that would hold me so tightly yet tenderly to his naked chest with a scent that aroused me like never before. Someone to make love to me when the time came that would caress me, loving me, exploring each other's bodies; showing affection in a special kind of way and caring about pleasing me more than himself. Just like a scene straight out of the movies. I fantasized how romantic it would be—a candlelight dinner at an elegant hideaway, a favorite song to always remember while slow dancing in each other's arms. Then I would return to reality, to the world I found myself in with so many mixed feelings, and I couldn't quite imagine just how Charles would ask me. I had dropped subtle hints as to what type of ring I would really love to have. But I knew deep down not wanting to believe that it would be a choice that the Queen would make, not what I wanted.

With Christmas just around the corner, I still hoped a ring—the beautiful diamond ring that I had dreamed of—would be my Christmas present. I smiled from ear to ear as the enchantment overwhelmed me.

Christmas was here! Would it really happen? Charles was on his way. He was in town for a long weekend. I could see his car coming up the long winding dirt driveway that led to my house. I could hardly control my excitement. I had missed him so much. It seemed that when he was away for several weeks at a time it calmed some of my mixed emotions and fears. He could be quite a smooth talker over the phone, controlling and manipulating my way of thinking to suit him. In spite of all that, I just knew this would be the greatest Christmas ever. He opened the car door and stepped out. Immediately, I was there in his arms. I greeted him with a passionate kiss and then we went in to be with my family. I had not revealed my thoughts or excitement of an engagement ring to anyone. After dinner, the family gathered to exchange gifts. He had not entered with a package or a gift. This was confirmation that I was right. He had the ring concealed in his pocket and he was going to propose in front of my entire family. I beamed with unspeakable happiness. Everyone was gathered around for the opening of their gifts, which had already begun.

"Oh, I need to retrieve your gift from the car," he said and excused himself. In a moment he re-entered carrying a medium size box.

My heart sank.

"This is for you."

Still hopeful, I began to unwrap the gift. Inside was apparel. An older lady's ugly jacket and pants set. Certainly not my style at all. Really, Charles? Really!

"I hope you like it. My mom picked it out," he explained with no emotion.

"Like it? Of course, I like it."

I knew all too well this was just another tactic of his mother's sardonic controlling innovation. She had obviously derailed any notion that he entertained regarding placing a ring on my finger. I could hardly get the words out. The disappointment overtook me. I wanted so much to cry. That was the first time I learned to cry without tears, but it would certainly not the last. He only stayed for a short while longer and left expressing how tired he was after just driving in from South Georgia earlier in the day.

"But you just got here less than an hour ago," I pleaded. "I've not seen you in three and a half weeks and suddenly you must go. But why and what is more important?" I asked, so frustrated and embarrassed.

"I have something I need to do. I'll call you later."

"But you haven't even gotten your gift from me."

"Oh, I'll get it later. It's no big deal," he said, as he hurriedly got in the car and closed the door.

In my saddened and confused state, I was ready for him to go. He quickly kissed me goodbye through the opened window and went on his way. I slowly went back inside with my family and wished all my family a Merry Christmas with a hug and a kiss.

"Good night, Baby Girl. Merry Christmas," Daddy said as he stood with a hug and a smile.

I excused myself to my room. As I took one more look at the hideous gift, suddenly the feelings I had felt the first day I met Charles' mother came rushing over me. She had sent a message to me with this gift.

"You are cheap and not worthy of my son. I am in control!" I could hear her screaming at me.

As I stood in the silence of my bedroom, the knock on the door startled me back to reality.

"Sandra? Sandra, are you ok, Hun?" Mama's loving voice softly spoke on the other side of the door.

I opened the door and Mama gave me a big hug as she often did and told me how much she loved me before turning to go to her room for the night. I sensed that Mama had noticed my disappointment, but she did not question me. Being a wise Mama, she knew that when I was ready, I would come to her and share. I was so thankful to have such a loving family as I realized this was not the case for all people.

Charles did not come to see me anymore through the Christmas holiday. He phoned the next night to say he was driving back to South Georgia because work had called for him to come back.

"I'll call you later."

Several weeks later, Charles came home again for a weekend visit. He was talking to me about the future, our future.

"Why do you talk about our future, Charles? You haven't asked me to marry you and you haven't given me a ring. Do you know how embarrassing that is for me? I tell people we are going to build a future together and they ask to see my ring. Really, Charles," I tried to express softly without upsetting him.

He was suddenly withdrawn and very displeased. He had nothing at all to say about anything I had said. It was not like me to share my thoughts or deep feelings like this.

He took in a deep breath, held it for a few moments, then exhaled. He could not let go of his explosive anger just yet. Not until he had sealed this commitment, and I was truly his to own. He would continue to hide his true deepest evil array of colors until I could not escape and would have to endure whatever he saw fit to unleash on me.

Ten

On the next weekend visit, Charles arrived and surprised me.

"Get ready. We are going to look at rings," he said with no emotion at all in his voice.

Once again, I was beside myself. All the disappointment and hurt just faded, evaporated, as quickly as it had appeared. And looked was all we did, just looked. I had left so sure I would be coming home with a ring, but that was not the case. So excited, yet very reserved so as not to rock the boat with Charles.

"This is no big deal," he expressed total disinterest in this venture.

On arrival at the jewelry store, I tried hard to contain myself as far as showing my excitement to be marrying this tall handsome guy standing beside me. He did all the talking. I thought this part would be easy, having dreamed about the perfect ring so many times.

"Hi, how can I help you?" the girl behind the counter asked.

"We are looking for rings," he replied.

The girl turned to me. "What kind of ring do you have in mind?"

I had already spotted it. "The wide band with the solitaire diamond in the second row."

"No, do not bring that ring out, because she does not deserve a ring like that ring."

I felt like a mac truck had hit me in the chest. Barely able to breathe, I turned and looked at him to see if maybe he was joking.

"I am sure you deserve a ring like that," he said, flirting with the girl. He had that big, inappropriate grin plastered across his face.

"If you see a ring you'd like for me to have, then you pick one," I said.

"You may get a ring; you may not," he teased.

The inappropriate grin remained on his face and was now imprinted in my memory forever. This was supposed to be such a wonderful experience to be shared for a lifetime. At least that was the way it was in my dreams. I could hardly hold back the tears and excused myself to wait outside the store. When he was done talking, laughing and flirting with the girl in the store he came out, of course with no ring. Beyond humiliated and heartbroken that he would insult me in such a way, I remained silent as Charles drove me home. What kind of man is this? What was I doing planning to spend my life with him? Realizing this was once again a mind game that Charles' mother had taught him to play so well. Would his mother be the one to have the final say in which ring I would wear as his wife, or if I would even get one?

Three weeks later, Charles arrived for his routine weekend visit. He had picked me up about twelve to go get a bite to eat down the road at the Pizza Place. He never really appeared to be excited to see me. As a matter of fact, he showed little, if any, emotion about anything up until this point. A short distance down the driveway; he stopped the car and handed me a tiny box.

"Here, here is your ring," he blurted out, expressing aggravation in his voice.

As I cautiously opened the box, once again I was disappointed. He had presented me with a ring. A ring that resembled nothing like the ones that I had so excitedly pointed out to him, but it was quite the opposite. Where was the romance? Where was the fantasy I had dreamed of from my knight in shining armor? Yes, the dark-headed woman who lived in the mysterious house must have had a hand in this, too. But I was becoming an expert at hiding my tears and disappointment from Charles. Little did I know that he enjoyed the control he had over me and he had no doubt of the times he was disappointing me. Blinded to it all, my feelings of sadness that he needed someone to love him because he wasn't even loved by his own mother seemed to overrule my personal feelings. I placed his feelings and lack of love as a priority far above my own and thought that showing him love would make it all up to him. I could fix it. How could I be so tantalized by him? I was a very smart girl. Why had I accepted this assignment to right all the wrong of this dysfunctional, demented person? What blinded me?

I put the ring on my finger. He reached over and gave me a peck of a kiss on the cheek. Was this really happening this way or was I going to wake from this nightmare?

At the end of the pizza date, he drove me straight back home, never mentioning the ring again. He let me out and said he needed to go.

"I'll talk to you later," he said as he reached over and gave me a peck of a kiss.

I watched as he backed up the car and left. I did not see Charles the next day. I would frequently look at the engagement ring and wonder why I felt such an obligation to remain in this relationship. I obviously had fallen under his manipulative trance to allow myself to be taken captive like this. I felt I had no say in my own life. Was I substituting empathy for true love? Was he playing me toward that path? At the end of the weekend, Charles returned to South Georgia to work, and the weeks flew by. Why had Charles chosen me for this role? What was his reasoning? I wasn't wealthy. I was not a socialite. I did not have connections in high or low places. I was just a simple country girl. Maybe he thought I was so naïve that he could use me as a gofer. What was his plan and where did I fit in? He had obviously researched my history and all about my family from the beginning. But why?

Three days later Charles phoned and informed me I could set an official date for the wedding. With such mixed emotions, knowing that I had no escape because of the information that Charles had intentionally shared with me for that distinct purpose, there was no inner enthusiasm. I set the date for six months down the road. I needed more time. Charles wasn't interested in helping plan the wedding at all. He didn't care where or when it happened. He just wanted to seal the commitment with someone he could punish, as a substitute for his mother. I busily attended several wedding showers and parties that relatives on both sides sponsored. There were so many beautiful expensive gifts given. I was overjoyed and thankful, nothing was taken for granted. It was so hard to conceal the innermost regret hidden deep within and present a "so happy" visible persona.

It was only a few months until the big day. Mama and I had shopped together looking for the perfect wedding dress. We shopped several stores hoping to find just the right one. She sat so proudly as I modeled each selection. I tried to stay within a reasonable price range, knowing she would do her best to get the one I really wanted. I had such a peace whenever we were together. She was my very best friend, never judging me, even in my mistakes she understood me. She made me feel so secure with just the touch of her hand. She was always there for me, no matter what. We talked every day without fail and I loved hearing her sweet voice on the other end of the line. I was their only girl. Mama and Daddy worked so hard to make sure I would have the most perfect wedding. These memories with my parents were by far the most treasured of my wedding memories.

Eleven

The rain was beating down on the windshield, lightning lighting up the entire sky, thunder roaring with huge crashes of sound. Charles and I were on a date. It was only four months before we were to be wed. He drove onto the long dirt driveway that was a quarter of a mile from the old farmhouse. He turned the car motor off and, out of nowhere, proceeded to inform me of my status.

"No other man will ever give you a second look. You belong to me. I want you, now!"

So taken by surprise at the tone in his voice, fear welled up in me. He quickly ripped down my panties, as not to give me a chance to respond with objection. He had already unzipped his zipper and unclothed himself quickly. At first, he was tender and easy as he placed himself on top of me. I was voicing disapproval.

"No. Please, just wait. I'm not ready! No, please."

He ignored me completely. I trembled as the impending uncertainty darkened the moment. Scared was an understatement. Being my first time, I had not a clue of what this experience should be like or how it should feel. But the one thing I did know was that this was not the way that I wanted it to be. I wanted to wait until our wedding night as Charles would sweep me up in his arms and carry me across the threshold and would gently, lovingly, and passionately make love to me. My knight in shining armor would complete me in such a sensuous way.

"No, please, just wait. I'm not ready! No, please," I repeated.

"You belong to me, no one else. You are going to like this."

He was on top of me. There was no longer any tenderness from him. His breathing accelerated. The evil ambience was suddenly there in the car with us. I pleaded. The emotions of horrific doom swept over me. Terrified, the apprehension of danger surrounded me. But there was no one to help. No way out. The more I protested, the harder and harder he thrust. Again and again, he thrusted harder each time. He lunged his full weight upon me. Immobilized under the weight that had me pinned down, there was no freeing myself. He was bigger. He was stronger. I struggled, pushing and wrestling for freedom to no avail. Trying to distract him I tried to jerk free one last time. I began to cry—begging and pleading.

"Please, stop. You are hurting me. Please, please stop."

I felt as though my flesh was being torn, ripped apart. There was a burning sensation as though someone was holding a branding iron inside of me. The piercing pain made me want to vomit. The more I cried, the louder he laughed and the harder he thrust. I continued to plead as though I was pleading for my life. Finally, it was over. He had climaxed and rolled off me. Totally exhausted and motionless, I could not move. His touch was cold and cruel. He placed his clothing back on as though he had just won his biggest trophy ever, never speaking a word, just that horrible echoing laugh. He had that inappropriate smile that radiated across his face as if to say, "I'm in control."

I was in so much pain—excruciating, piercing, and stabbing—I could hardly move. I sat speechless with my head turned away from Charles, staring into the deep, dark night. Torn between the love I felt for this man, the morals I was taught by Grandmama, and the feelings that this was not supposed to feel this way, I silently questioned what just happened to me? Jesus, help me! Please help me. I wanted to run but the pain was paralyzing. I had no strength to get away. The rain continued to beat down hard upon the car as the noise of the windshield wipers moving back and forth across the windshield amplified. The lightning and thunder became more intense. And now shaking uncontrollably on the inside, I knew this could not be right. He was very cold and distant, as though I was just an object to him. He exhibited no signs of guilt or remorse for the act that he had just committed. As I sat shocked and gazing out the window, the excruciating pain became unbearable. This was a side of Charles I had never seen before, a sinister side that he seemed to lavish. I looked around to locate my panties that he had ripped off me. As I bent to retrieve them from the floorboard of the car, I suddenly felt an unusual amount of wetness between my shaking legs. I was trembling all over, frightened, feeling violated, afraid to say anything for fear of making him angry. I kept quiet. He cranked the car and backed out of the driveway without saying a word. Oh, God, I just want to go home, my heart prayed.

"Please, just take me home, Charles," I begged in a soft voice.

"No! Not yet, not like this."

I had just been violently raped by a stranger, a man that I did not even know. What was he going to do to me now? As he drove down the back country roads, I was feeling weaker and weaker. I tried hard to stay calm. I did not want to upset him. I just wanted him to take me home.

"Please, Charles, will you turn the inside light on for just a minute?" I asked softly.

He insisted, in an abrupt tone, on knowing why I needed the light on as he simultaneously turned it on. I was covered in blood. My heart was racing, I knew that I would not last long with this amount of blood gushing out without ceasing. I quivered unable to control what was happening to me. As I raised my leg to investigate where the blood was coming from it squirted all the way to the dash with a force behind it. I was close to a weakened state of passing out because of the amount of blood loss. I begged him to take me home.

"I need help. Please, just take me home," I continued, begging frantically. I was fighting hard to stay alert, but was losing the fight slowly.

He harshly yelled, "No! Bleeding is normal for the first time."

I had enough nurse training to know that this much blood was not normal. I was getting weaker and weaker. I knew I was dying. Hardly able to keep my eyes open, I could feel my heart slowing. Was he so vain that he was going to let me die?

"I am going to take you to a friend's house to get cleaned up. They will understand," he said nonchalantly.

He drove another ten or fifteen minutes to his friend's house. A friend he'd never mentioned before. I was fading in and out of consciousness as he rang the doorbell. No one answered. All the lights were off, and it was more than apparent no one was there. He just returned to the car, looked at me in disgust as though this was all my fault, yet he said nothing. He backed the car out of the drive, screeching the tires as he straightened to drive away.

"Please, Charles, take me to the hospital. I can call Dr. Sam, a friend of Grandmama's. He will help me. Please, Charles," I pleaded. "I promise never to tell anyone what happened. Please, Charles, don't let me die," I begged as my strength was fading quickly. "I am going to die if you do not get me help. Please, Charles, I don't want to die."

Only able to beg at a whisper now, I felt that there was no use to even try. He was not going to get me help. He was above taking any responsibility for any wrong that had been done. After riding around for another fifteen or twenty minutes, I became unresponsive. In a panic, he finally gave in and drove me to the emergency room of a small hospital that was another thirty minutes away.

"Sandra, can you hear me? You are not to tell anyone! Do you hear me?" Charles whispered in my ear, as he lifted me out of the car.

On my arrival to the emergency room, I was semi-conscious and was placed on a stretcher immediately as nurses rushed around quickly. My uncontrollable shaking mimicked a seizure. I could not stop. The trembling was continuous. The pain was so intense my body had shut down into a state of shock. I could faintly hear the nurses frantically working around me. Feeling like my life was over, it was as if I was far, far away in the distance looking down. Too weak to even try to survive, I closed my eyes. Where was Charles? What would he tell my parents? If I lived or if I died, what would he tell my parents? This was not at all what I had imagined making love with this man that I had yearned for so very much would be like. As I looked around, coming in and out of consciousness, I saw that my nail beds were already blue, and I had no recordable blood pressure. Slipping further and further away, I could hear the nurses telling me to stay with them.

"Come on, Sandra! Hang in there! Stay with us," one of the older nurses kept repeating. The nurses were busily discussing what had happened to cause this tragedy. One was so sure I was having a miscarriage. I was so weak I could not even defend myself to tell them this was my first time to have sex. There was no baby to miscarry. But they went on and on with their judgmental opinions of my condition.

Oh, God, forgive me, I prayed silently. Please, Lord, don't let Mama and Daddy think badly of me. Please, Lord. Oh, and Grandmama, Lord. I love them so much. I prayed quietly as I floated in and out. Suddenly I heard my Mama's voice and a shrill cry.

"Oh, my God, help my baby girl!" Mama's scream propelled.

The sheet that covered me was saturated with blood. It was the third one the nurse had placed over me. Blood was everywhere. The blood just continued to saturate each new sheet.

"I am sorry, Ma'am," the nurse informed Mama, "but we must be going. We are headed straight to surgery. The doctor will come out to the waiting area after the surgery and speak with you and your husband."

"But what is wrong? Why is she going to surgery?" Mama asked with panic in her voice.

"We have got to stop the bleeding right away," the nurse called back to Mama. "We do not yet know the cause."

As they wheeled me down the hall, I could hear Mama praying in a faraway muffled voice. Would I come back to my Mama and Daddy? At this point, it was critical. It was very doubtful that I would survive. Mama and Daddy stood at the end of the hall as the nurses quickly rolled me out of sight. My life was hanging only by a thread. No one had seen Charles since he had dropped me off and made a phone call to my parents to tell them I was at the hospital. He had offered no explanations to anyone. And he certainly felt no obligation to offer any.

Twelve

I awoke in a frantic state—screaming and so scared. It was such a cold, dark, shivering, quiet place. I could hear no one around me. Not able to fully wake up, I was trying so hard. Was I alive or had I died? I was just not sure at this point. The pain struck me. Agonizing, grueling, piercing pain. I was quivering and shivering, as though I was in an ice bucket covered from head to toe. I had no idea what had really happened to me. I remembered the heavy weight of Charles' body on top of me and how I struggled to breathe underneath the weight. I remembered begging for my life. I remembered the fury, the disgust, the nonchalant attitude of Charles. He seemed to relish in my begging, my pain, my fear, and him having control of my life in his hands. He could get me help or he could let me die. The evil persona that was present at the mystery house on the hill was relentless, as far as he was concerned. It seemed to be hidden deep within him. But what had happened to me? Was I alive?

"Wake up, sweetheart," a nurse standing over me softly spoke. "You are in the recovery room. You are fine, Sandra. Can you hear me? Open your eyes, now."

The anesthesia had not worn off completely. I had been at the hospital for six hours. The procedure was a lengthy one, requiring extreme expertise and assistance from the Master Surgeon. Mama had prayed without ceasing. She had a direct line to God. I had been in the operating room for five and a half hours. Were my family and Charles waiting together outside the double doors? My parents could not imagine what had happened to their only daughter. But immoral behavior was never an option for them. What had Charles told them? The doctor approached me as I struggled to wake up. I had made it. I was alive. The doctor sat beside the stretcher on which I lay and began explaining what had happened to me. He held my hand and spoke with nonjudgmental gentleness, as though he knew of the torture and abuse that I had experienced and how frightened I must have been.

"Charles penetrated through your vagina and through the abdominal wall, severing the main artery with his penis. Another five minutes, Sandra, and you would not have survived," he said with eyes full of empathy.

He explained to me that this time it was the Master Surgeon that had intervened, and that was the only reason I had survived. My eyes welled with tears, still very weak and in pain.

"Thank you, Doctor. Thank you, Jesus, that I am still here," I spoke softly.

My concern immediately turned to my parents. How they must be frantic, out of their minds with worry. They must never know what had really happened. I could not hurt them like this. Their daughter would never have allowed something like this. I was already blaming myself for what had happened. And Charles; what would Daddy do to him if he knew he had raped his baby girl? He would beat him within an inch of his life, so he could suffer for a while, then die. But then I would be without my Daddy. No, they must never know. I would live with this secret forever.

"Please, Doctor, don't tell my parents," I pleaded for one more miracle.

The surgeon once again took my hand and looked into my weak, pale blue eyes.

"Sweetheart, that is your decision alone," he said. "You are almost nineteen years old. That is your choice."

Then I drifted out again. The doctor exited the recovery room to find Mama and Daddy right outside the double doors. They had been waiting for five and a half long, agonizing hours.

"I have good news," he assured them. "Sandra is going to be okay. I have only heard of one other case like this in my career of many years, and they did not make it. The credit goes to the Master Surgeon."

Then he turned and shook Daddy's hand and patted Mama on the shoulder. He knew she was a praying mother. That was obvious to anyone who met her. When my parents asked what had happened, all he said was, "A blood vessel had ruptured."

The week before, I had received my premarital exam. It was very painful for me because at that time I was still very much a virgin. Mama had accompanied me to that appointment. She knew that it was difficult for me and that there had been a little bleeding afterwards. Mama reasoned that having that exam must have caused this to happen.

Charles was not there in the waiting area as the surgeon spoke to my parents. My brother and his wife had seen him rushing away from the hospital earlier, headed for his vehicle as if on a mission to clean a crime scene. He did not know if I would survive or not. But he would have never accepted responsibility for his actions or my death. Little did Charles know, but on their way into the hospital my brother and his wife had passed by his vehicle. They had seen all the blood inside. The blood that he was hurrying to get rid of as well as dispose of my bloody clothing that was left in the vehicle on my arrival the night before. That was evidence that he had let me bleed for a long while before getting me the help I needed. My brother and his wife, Iris, had already concluded that there was more to this story from all the blood and the bloody handprints where I had so desperately held on through the exorbitant pain as I was fighting for my life.

I awakened in the ICU several hours later. My first thought was of my parents. What had they been told? I had such mixed feelings about Charles. It was only a few months before the wedding. How could I get out of it? Gifts had been given, invitations sent, promises made. And now, this! I did not even know who he was when he so brutally abused and raped me. The pleasure he took in my pain as I begged him to stop was like a greater climax for him, a driving force for him to inflict as much hurt as he could to prove he was in charge. He had a boiling fury inside him that stemmed from the deepest pits of hell. There was a black fire that burned in his eyes as the inappropriate smile lit up across his face. I shook, quivering to the innermost part of my soul as I remembered.

Visitation to the ICU was not open for another two hours. The family waited anxiously to see me. Charles had returned and paced back and forth, trying to portray the concerned hero that had saved my life. I wanted to see my parents so badly. But ironically, he was the first one in to see me when the doors opened for visitation. He had insisted on visiting first. I trembled as he came toward me. He bent down over me. His expression tight. He spoke with military authority, his voice like a rushing wind in my ear.

"Sandra, you are not to reveal any details of the night before! Do you understand?" he spoke through gritted teeth. "Even though it was your fault. If you had not fought, if you had just laid still." Charles hurriedly and matter-of-factly whispered in my ear.

In his way of thinking, he had done nothing wrong. If I had only cooperated, none of this would have happened. He was so consumed with controlling the situation he never even considered my condition. Was I out of harm's way? After all, I was still in the ICU. It was never about me, only protecting himself. He did not care about my condition, only about controlling the situation as it illuminated his stance. A strategy used often as a defense mechanism for someone like Charles with low self-esteem. He was the best of the best at turning things around and making me question myself. He was great at convincing me that it was always my fault, no matter what the issue was. I began to vomit, my pain increasing, and my vital signs elevated with the threat that was being given to me with that inappropriate smile across his face. The nurse caring for me entered the room.

"I am sorry, but you will have to leave now," she said politely. She easily assessed that he was the reason for the sudden change in my condition.

"Please, I need to see my parents," I cried to the nurse. The nurse quickly escorted my parents to my bedside. They were so grateful that I was alive. They never questioned me. They gave Charles credit for saving my life. How could I ever tell them that he was the one responsible for almost ending my life. I must never let them know the real truth, I thought.

Thirteen

On the third day, I was dismissed from the ICU to a room on the fourth floor – Room 438. As the nurses turned the corner into the room, my eyes met with the eyes of Charles' mother. She stood there in all her eloquent, large and in charge presence. The notoriously inappropriate smile radiated from the corner where she stood. I suddenly realized what made this smile so inappropriate. It was a smile full of venom, as my Grandmama would say. I immediately cried out to the nurse.

"Where are my Mama and my Daddy?"

Before the nurse could answer, Charles' mother said, "I sent them home for some rest, Sandra. I met them earlier today, and they were totally exhausted. They have not left since you came here three days ago. Now, I promised I would take care of you." The Queen firmly stated.

"Where is Charles?"

"I sent him home to get some rest, too."

"Now, don't you worry about a thing. I am here to take care of you," she repeated.

Fear surmounted in me as she repeated those words, "take care of you." What had he told her? I was sure she was there to make certain I didn't accuse her beloved Charles of any wrongdoing. He had summoned her no doubt to be around to hear what I said or to prevent me from talking to anyone. I did not want to be left alone with the Queen of the mystery house that so beamed with the aura of evil all around her. Afraid, alarmed, agitated, anxious and uneasy was the way I felt all rolled up into just plain frantic. How could Mama let Charles' mother talk her into leaving? But then, Mama had no way of knowing, nor had she felt what I had felt emanating from this woman. It was as though she and Charles had some type of ability to get people to do things that they really didn't want to do without them even thinking it through. They had a knack for making it appear like they were doing others a great favor.

"Now, don't you worry, Honey. We are going to become the best of friends," she gloated.

After I was all situated in my new bed, the nurses went on to their other duties, leaving the call button within my reach. I lay quietly, momentarily distracted by thoughts of what Charles had revealed to his mother. I questioned myself. Was his mother there to do me more harm to protect her son? What was my life going to be like now? As soon as the nurse exited, the Queen rose and moved to the other side of my bed where the nurse had placed the call light.

"You won't be needing this, since I am here to take care of you," she smiled a threatening smile.

I never spoke, just listened.

"Now, I am sure you understand that my son has done nothing wrong in this situation," she paused to straighten the sheets. "And if you decide to try to hold it over his head and manipulate him with any threats of any kind, I will see to it that not only will you be destroyed, but your family as well."

She reminded me of the gifts already given and the wedding showers that had already been planned. "You are not going to humiliate me by making up some preposterous story about the events of that unfortunate evening. Understood?"

I lay in silence and nodded my head.

"So, from here on, we will pretend to be best of friends," the Queen in all her glory had spoken.

This was a solid confirmation of what I knew I felt the first time I met this woman. She was evil and straight from the deepest pits of hell. And she loved to be center stage in this play of life, especially her son's life.

Four days later, I was dismissed from the hospital. Charles, the "hero" had come to drive me home. My parents gave their approval, not knowing that this was not what I wanted. How could they have known? They would meet me at home. Still torn between love and fear, I was reserved and frigid. On the way home there was little to say. Afraid that anything I said would provoke his fury, I thought it was better to just keep quiet. He broke the silence.

"I've received another transfer," he said staring straight ahead. "I will be going even farther into South Georgia for several weeks. I'll call and come home on the weekends when I can. I may not get to come home as often because it is farther away, but I will call," he rambled on.

Remaining silent, I was so confused about what had happened to me. My beliefs that sex before marriage was wrong overwhelmed me with shame. The one thing I was sure of was that this was not the man I wanted to marry. But now, having been raped by him, he had convinced me that no one else would ever want me. He had reminded me several times that no man would give me a second look. He made me feel so unclean, so violated, repeatedly with his hateful words. I was relieved in a way that Charles was going farther away and maybe I would not see him for a while.

I was so unsure of what my future held after this. Would I be able to ever have sex again? Would I ever want to? The fear, the pain, the thought of someone touching me like that again was a constant companion. How would I, or could I, get beyond these feelings? And what about the issue of having children? Would I be able to have children? All these feelings and questions I pondered over and over during the twenty-mile ride from the hospital to home. Reliving the episode of that night in my mind was as if I was watching someone else's life being changed forever at the hands of an evil, irrational, self-absorbed human being. I felt trapped and obligated to marry a man I now deeply feared and resented. I felt disgust when I looked at him now, so I tried to look straight through him instead.

When I broke the silence trying to explain to him that I still felt physically weak and drained, the usual ridiculing, criticizing and obscenities emerged as if he were speaking to his mother. It was as if another personality suddenly appeared, one I had met only once before. I quickly learned to keep quiet.

As time went by, I physically recuperated from the act of love making that was so violently forced on me, almost ending my life. Emotionally, I was more devastated than ever. I remained torn with what the future would hold for me, if I indeed married this man—the man I thought would be the lover of my dreams. I had always envisioned my dream lover on one knee with a sparkling diamond ring telling me that I was the love of his life and how much he adored me. Just the look on his face would set the fire of desire inside me uncontrollably ablaze. At that moment I would say "yes," and from that point in time, we would be the happiest two people in the world. This was a reoccurring dream that I often had, but Charles was never in the dream. Another warning that I failed to recognize.

Several weeks later, I received a discharge from my surgeon, a man that had been so caring and kind to me. He had inquired on my last visit to him about the events that led up to me being brought to the hospital. He was concerned and his advice to me was what I already knew.

"This is not the way that someone treats someone they love," he said. "This act was in no way about his love for you. It was instead a substitution for punishment of another. This is a sick person with whom you are dealing." The doctor expressed this advice firmly, yet in a genuinely concerned way. "The next time, Sandra, you may not be as fortunate; you may not survive," he added, with furrowed brow.

I already knew that in my heart. "Thank you, Doctor, for saving my life. I will find a way out."

With God's help there must be a way out, I assured myself silently. I had heard others speak with very judgmental attitudes against women who stayed in abusive, dysfunctional relationships, but I never dreamed I would be one of those on the receiving end of abuse. "Why do they stay?" some would ask. As though it was such an easy decision. But there are tons of reasons why someone in an abusive or dysfunctional relationship can't leave. The majority of women claim love is the answer. However, in my case, that was certainly not true. Charles had already destroyed any ounce of love that I thought I ever had for him. From the outside looking in, I'm sure my actions seemed to be questionable. Why not just leave? Why ignore the signs, when there were so many? Never does abuse limit itself to the confines of one environment, but it affects a scope of many. And the decisions of the abused can tilt the scale toward life or death. But then again, I guess it was for love—the love of my family—that I stayed.

Fourteen

Three months later, the night before my wedding, I lay awake. Knowing, without a doubt, that I was about to make the biggest mistake of my life and knowing there was nothing I could do about it. I had pondered night after night all the scenarios of what it would be like if I suddenly canceled the wedding. The words of the Queen echoed in I mind over and over.

"I will destroy not only you, but your family as well."

I had morally committed myself when I allowed Charles to take advantage of me on that stormy, life-threatening night months ago. Even though he was twice my size and there was no way I could have managed to escape from underneath him, I consumed the blame. Now the consequences; payment for the rest of my life. Of that, I was certain.

The wedding day was not far away, and the Queen requested an audience with me. She was always so dramatic, as if she was competing for an Oscar. She sat me down at the kitchen table and tried to convince me not to marry Charles. She declared that he was a bad person with mental issues. As I listened, I was blown away by what she was saying. I came to the conclusion that any mother who could speak to and treat their own child the way she had her son, must be straight from Satan. I realized that it was the Queen who had made him the way he was. What was she trying to do? She did not want me to cancel the wedding, yet now she was attempting to persuade me not to marry him. The Queen was notorious for swaying back and forth with Charles. This turned out to be just another strategy of hers to stress me, because she had already threatened me, and she knew I was trapped after all that had happened. Was she now realizing the reality that he would not be there under her roof for her enjoyment? Had he said something or done something that had infuriated her to this point? I had no way of knowing. I trusted no one, especially the Queen of the mystery house. But it was too late. I knew I had no choice but to marry him, because I continually felt the threat against my family and myself was very real. Being so unsure of her motives, I felt that her actions were unpredictable as she directed our lives in this direction. I knew she had written another act to her play.

Now more convinced than ever that the family that lived on the secluded hill had a lot more hidden secrets than I could ever imagine, I cringed at the thoughts of what Charles might have endured at the hands of this woman, the Queen. He seemed to be defenseless against her, even though they would exchange words that should never be shared between a child and parent. He acted as though he despised her, yet she would still win control of his thinking and manipulate him without him even realizing it. Or could it be that she knew something he had done or was involved in and was using it to control and manipulate him to do whatever she instructed?

I was all alone in this. I could not share with him what the Queen had been trying to do. I was caught between the two most evil people I had ever known. How would I ever survive? Or would I be able to?

Fifteen

Everyone said I was a lovely bride. My father, whom I adored, escorted me down the aisle to give me away to a man that even he had reservations about. He never spoke of his innermost doubts, but I knew him well enough that he didn't have to express them out loud. I stepped up to the altar to meet this lifetime partner, a charming, handsome, dark stranger that also had a deep dark side. He was so debonair that he hid things very well from others. In their eyes he was the hero. The knight in shining armor that had saved my life.

I had only gotten a glimpse of this dark side four months ago as I begged for my life on that dark stormy night. If only all my friends could just see inside my heart. I wanted so badly to run and hide. I trembled with fear unsure of what the future held. Would I survive? Would I even live? I loved my family more and the risk was just too great. I did not have a choice but to remain.

Charles and I left the reception hall as our family and friends wished us well. Off to our honeymoon spot in Gatlinburg, Tennessee. I should have been elated, but I had a sickening feeling deep down inside. A grotesque captivation lingered from that night, the night that changed everything for me. I was alone now for the first time since that night with the man that had almost cost me my life and then threatened me if I told anyone. I sat quietly as he drove. Prolonged periods of silence stagnated the surroundings as he drove into the night. Finally arriving at our hotel, I waited in the car for him to check us in.

"Got it," he said as he entered the car.

"Great," I replied, with a fake smile.

Inside of me, the tension, anxiety, apprehension and the instilled fear was at an all-time high. Would I live through the next few hours that were supposed to be the one of the greatest times of my life, or would I once again knock on heaven's door? Again, silence filled the space. Charles opened the door to the hotel room and motioned for me to go inside. Certainly not the picture that I had fantasized about while waiting for my dream knight in shining armor to appear in my life. Being carried across the threshold with excitement and laughter, romantic lust and passion was certainly out of the question. He had proven that he was in control four months ago. He knew I feared him and he loved it. He drooled on the fact that I had married him, even with this surmountable instilled fear that seemed to heighten each time we were together. I had managed not to be alone with him since that night. But now "I was his wife," he boasted with such ego as if he were a famous fighter that had won after the kill. He stripped immediately and lay out across the bed.

"Come on!" he said in a demanding tone.

"I need to freshen up, Charles," I offered timidly. "We have been driving for hours without stopping."

We had not even stopped to eat, because he wanted to drive straight through. We would eat when he said so, no matter how hungry I was.

"Well, hurry up," he ordered.

I entered the bathroom and locked the door behind me. I was shaking all over, cold and clammy, my stomach was in knots. I had flashes back to that night—the pain, the excruciating pain, the blood, the begging—it all rushed through my mind over and over. This would be the first time since that night. What if he rapes me again? What if he is so rough like before that he hurts me? What if he tears through my vagina again, and makes me bleed? I am so far from home. Would he let me die this time? Like a whirlwind these thoughts and questions coiled confusion and terror through my whole body. I procrastinated as long as I could. He had turned the TV on and the volume up very loud. He was yelling through the door above the sound of the television.

"What's taking you so long?" he yelled in a frustrated tone.

"I'll be right out," I called back.

I turned off the lights and opened the bathroom door. I was donned in a black negligee that was so beautiful. Trembling, nauseated, scared and so disappointed in myself for allowing this situation to escalate to the point of marriage. Charles and his mother were two of a kind. He was the spitting image of a woman that I knew had a hidden demeanor, capable of doing things that I could not even imagine, because it was not in me to be that cruel or that evil. The Queen was a woman to be feared and I was beginning to see that he might just be the same. They shared a very unusual relationship, more of a hate/hate relationship than a love/hate relationship. Love was not a word that the Black family knew at all. I knew that I not only had him to reckon with but also his mother. He had fallen asleep and snored every other breath or so. I quietly sat down on the floor in front of the television and sat with my knees pulled up to my chest. I was mulling the same thoughts over and over. What have I gotten myself into? This is such a mistake. I want to go home to my Mama and Daddy. Tears welled up in my eyes.

Suddenly, Charles woke up in such an angry state he immediately grabbed my arm. His grip was furious, catching me completely off guard. He pulled me up on the bed by one arm. I was petrified.

"What do you mean?" he shouted. "I didn't drive all this way for you to sit and watch TV." His face was red and the veins on his neck bulged.

"But you were asleep," I tried to explain, tears cascading down my face. "I was trying to let you rest."

The pain in my right arm throbbing as the swelling and bruising had already started to invade the tissue underneath his forceful grip. In a rage, he slapped me across the face and instructed me in a harsh voice.

"Pull that thing off. You are my wife now and you will do what I say. Do you understand?"

"Yes," I tried to say without emotion.

He then mounted me in a raw kind of way. No tenderness, no love, just an animal instinct kind of act. I just lay there stiff with the fear of dying. It was so painful again. He thrust his extra-large penis into me as if it were some kind of punishment. He had to know he was hurting me. The full weight of his body on me like before was crushing me to the point I could not breathe. As I squirmed to try to push him off to catch a breath, he pinned my wrist to the bed and thrust repeatedly. Then he laughed.

"Please, Charles, please you are hurting me," I cried, gasping for air.

He got more excited with every plea I made. It seemed to heighten his climax to induce more pain and hear me beg him to stop. He loved to see me cry, making himself feel superior. Finally, it was over. He had climaxed and rolled off me. I lay there stunned, not sure what to do. Was the wetness between my legs blood? Was I going to die? Finally, I asked for permission to go the bathroom.

"Yeah, sure," he responded despondently. Charles acted completely oblivious to the emotions I was struggling with. He knew this was the first time since that tragic night. He did not express any concern or caring in trying to reassure me that he would not hurt me again. Instead, he was exhilarated by the fact that he had induced such pain and fear within me. I rushed into the bathroom and sat on the cold floor crying silently, so he could not hear me. I would learn quickly to cry without tears in his presence, because tears seem to give him enjoyment in his bizarre behavior. I did not know what to do. Should I call my Daddy? No, no, I could not do that. Daddy had made a promise to Charles before we married.

"If you ever lay a hand on her to hurt her," Daddy said. "I will beat you to your death."

No, I did not want Daddy to go to jail. And Daddy loved me that much. He would not hesitate to beat Charles, just like he told him he would. I waited in the bathroom until I could hear him snoring deeply. His back was turned, and I gently lay down on the edge of the bed with my back to his. He had turned off the TV and the room was shadowy. I lay motionless, staring into the pitch-black darkness, paralyzed with the hopelessness of my impending doom at the hands of this stranger. I knew I could not confide in anyone what he had already done and certainly not what I feared the future might be like, if indeed, there was one. I was so far from home. What had I done that life would deal me such a harsh hand? I took nothing for granted. Just being innocent and naïve has led me to find myself in an inconceivable world of deception and evil.

The one night that was supposed to be one of laughter, romance and tender love where special memories were made, was one that I had rather forget. I had figured out early on that arguing or trying to express how I felt did not matter to Charles. It only provoked his anger and his need to exhibit his control, giving him opportunity to display his dark side. I decided that night to devote myself to making the best of an awfully dire situation. I would try to figure out how to make him happy. Maybe he didn't know how to be kind and loving because he never saw that in his home growing up. The mystery house that lured with such evil ambience was void of any type of love and affection.

As the sun rose early peeping through the window, I had exhausted myself to the point of sleep in the early morning hours. Now it was time to get up. I rolled over to find he was not there. I got up and looked around the room. I was alone and so hungry. We had not eaten since before the wedding. I quickly showered and got dressed, thinking he would be back any minute. There I sat all alone in fear. Wondering, doubting, questioning. Had he left and headed back home without me? Had I aroused more anger in him even as I slept? What hell was I to pay now? So, I waited patiently. This was all in the role of the play that Charles and his mother loved to perform: The Torturing Mind Games. Hours later he entered the room.

"I've missed you," I said lovingly, never questioning him or complaining.

He lay across the bed in silence. He never acknowledged that I had spoken. I then just sat quietly in fear on the other side of the room. He continued to lay there in silence. He would not even turn on the TV. Several hours later, he informed me that he was hungry, and I could go with him to get something to eat. There was silence all throughout the meal. I politely thanked him for my dinner. But there was no response from him.

The third day was just as miserable as the others. I was on pins and needles worried about saying the wrong thing that would trigger an outrage in him. I prayed that he would not touch me in a sexual way again. The thought of it was unsettling to say the least. He remained very distant in his own world. It seemed as though he was there all alone and I did not exist at all. Was this punishment for me? It was as though he was going through withdrawal from being away from the Queen. This was really a relief to me in a way. I was fine with him not touching me at all.

Sixteen

The three-day honeymoon was over. This was a far cry from the Hawaii honeymoon that Charles had told me that we would be taking. He had heard me speak of how I dreamed of going there someday. This was just another one of his manipulative deceiving acts that he played. He never had any intentions of taking me to Hawaii. These three days were three of the most miserable days of my life outside of the hospital ordeal and only the beginning of many, many more. Without giving reason for cutting the honeymoon short, we now would travel back home to our mobile home that was located on my parents' farm. I again kept quiet only speaking when he indicated that it was okay to do so. I had concluded that this was the way he liked it. He was not interested in anything I had to say.

As we traveled home, he had not shared with me that we would be detouring through Tennessee to pick up a car from his uncle's car dealership. Of course, this was another exploit of the Queen's to disrupt the time that he and I were to spend together. His mother had made arrangements for him to buy a vehicle there, leaving me to follow him home in her car that he had borrowed for our honeymoon. I did not protest, even though my feelings were confused once again, because I realized that it was the Queen that had dominated the way Charles had treated me from the beginning.

When we arrived at the car dealership, I was not introduced to anyone. I was instructed to remain in the car and keep quiet. I had an eerie feeling. What was really going on? This transaction seemed to be so secretive. I was definitely being kept in the dark. I was fighting a losing battle against such an evil spirit. This was our honeymoon. I could not understand how Charles could bow to such manipulation from his mother who treated him as if she hated him. It appeared that he only married me as a punishment to the Queen. Was that it? The answer to my question of why he chose me? Was it because he felt I was so simple he could manipulate me to his way of thinking and could use me easily? At what point and to what extent would he punish me again, pretending I was his mother? It was as though she controlled his every move. That is obviously where he learned to play the games he liked to play. The Queen once more was behind the scenes directing him and always interfering in how we should live and in every area of our lives. With mixed emotions I realized, however, she was unaware that for me this three-hour drive was a welcome reprieve from the insurmountable fear that his presence instilled in me.

Finally arriving home, I was relieved to be close to my family even though I could not share anything with them. Grandmama was not at all unaware of the fear and uneasiness that subsisted behind my facade of happiness. I focused on trying to be a good wife while finishing my nurse's training. I made sure my household chores were always completed before donating my time to my studying, caring for my animals or spending time with Grandmama, who lived just a stone's throw away from me.

Charles, on the other hand, seemed to devote his time to making sure I never became a nurse. He constantly criticized me.

"You are not smart enough to be a nurse," he mocked. "I know more about nursing than you will ever know."

He would try to hinder me in any way he could when it came to my studying or completing my assignments. He would keep me up at night before a big exam hoping to exhaust me to failure. Every time I would close my eyes in fatigue, Charles would slap my face and shake me.

"Look at me," he demanded. "Don't you close your eyes."

I would have to obey and force my eyes to stay open and on him. He would threaten me all through the night over things I knew absolutely nothing about. He would do this on a night that he was able to sleep late the next morning. But I took a strong stance on this issue. With only ten months left until graduation, I was not going to let anything stand in the way of my dream. A dream I had wanted since I was just a little child. I had lost one of my most important dreams, a husband that would adore me and love me for myself. I was not about to lose the third most important dream to me, to be a nurse. I was trying so hard to make the best of the situation. Maybe, if he thought I really cared and was trying to help him, things would change. I could only hope.

He made it very difficult for me to believe that my life would get better. Only a few days after returning from our honeymoon he insisted that I do something odd.

"You are to return all the gifts from your family that was given as wedding gifts."

"But Charles, why?" I questioned, immediately regretting that I did. "I love those gifts."

"You'll do as I say," he stated angrily. "Bring me every dime of the money you get back. Do you understand?"

I felt so sickened at this request, but I knew I had to obey him or I would pay dearly. In the meantime, I would express an outer happiness that just did not exist within me.

Seventeen

It was a very long drudging haul for me to complete my nurses training and make it to graduation; having gone through the traumatic experience of abuse and rape, my emotional roller coaster of a marriage, and the loss of my first-born child.

The sky darkened to a midnight stage; thunder rumbled in the far distance and lightning illuminated the sky over the entire farm. The surrounding atmosphere was gloomy to say the least, as I was alone in our 12 foot by 65 foot mobile home. I had prepared what I thought was a nutritious meal for Charles as he arrived home from work. But he did not see it that way. He hurried inside as if the rain would decompose him. He was grumbling as he entered our small home that I always kept immaculate. He often became malicious on his arrival home from work. I strived to be cautious not to ignite his anger, which happened often for what seemed to be no reason at all. I had worked to prepare his favorite dishes, hoping it would set the mood for a peaceful evening. But little did I know his favorite dishes had changed. He was not at all pleased.

"I've never liked these things," he bellowed. "You are trying to kill me with grease and fried crap like this." He was loud enough for Grandmama to hear next door.

I had prepared oven fried steak with gravy, cream potatoes and greens. He had requested this meal on several occasions. It was nothing for Charles to become violent in a split second. He pushed me down as I was trying to tell him I was sorry and would make him something else. As I rose to my feet, he spun me around again causing me to lose my balance. I hit the coffee table as I went down.

"Charles, please, you are going to hurt the baby. Charles, please."

He had his hand drawn back to hit me again. He suddenly stopped, then turned. Mumbling obscenities, he walked away. Thunder was overhead now, shaking the little mobile home with each loud clap. The lightning frequently streaked the midnight-colored sky, the rain and wind beat the tin roof aggressively. The mental abuse on this lonely, stormy night would have been enough to cause such devastation but the physical abuse as well was more than I could take. He went into the bedroom without eating anything. I quickly cleared away the meal I had prepared. Trembling, crying without tears, wondering what the night held in store, I knew I would have to pay before morning's light. A debt to be working to prepare a meal that I thought would be pleasing to my husband. It was all so confusing. How would I learn to please a man that was so unpredictable and manipulative? A man that had to control everything!

After the kitchen was cleaned, Charles remained in the bedroom with the door open. He lay masturbating to teach me a lesson. It was so humiliating for a grown man to act this way, to play these sickening games. I moved where I could not see him and never spoke a word. I sat down on the floor in front of the glass door and watched the pouring rain beat against the deck and the wind bend solid trees almost to a breaking point.

The lightning was continuously flashing across the entire sky. I sat holding my knees to my chest, again praying that he would just go away. Crying with hidden tears, I was so cold, so exhausted from the mind games and the fear of how he would decide to punish me. I prayed that God would give me the strength to endure this marriage, the understanding to help him. I so wanted him to be kind and loving. However, deep down, I knew that this was never going to happen. The damage had been done at the hands of the Queen many years ago and it was irreversible. The night seemed to be long, and I sat as still as I could, hoping not to draw attention from the bedroom where he had gone, I pretended that the quieter I was the greater the distance between me and Charles. Just maybe, he would not hurt me anymore tonight. I sat there silently crying, exhausted, terrified and trembling, as the rain beat down harder. Suddenly a piercing intense pain shot through my abdomen. My breathing accelerated. My fear heightened as the pain became so exaggerated, so sharp, it literally took my breath. Oh, no, God, no. My baby!

Fluid gushed from my vagina. Then, an all too familiar feeling of the thick sticky fluid that I had experienced before. The blood came gushing out. Oh my God, what is happening to me? I tried to move across the floor away from the door to where the phone was. The pain was so unbearable, I screamed when I moved. Was I going to lose the only thing that now made life worthwhile, my reason for living? Was I going to die? I came so close before. The bleeding, where was it coming from? Why so much blood? The scream was enough to bring Charles out of the bedroom to find me on the floor, my knees to my chest, tears streaming down my face, shaking uncontrollably, shivering and sobbing hysterically. I could not stop shaking, either from the thought of what was happening to me and my baby or the thought that Charles was there with me now. He was abrupt, not at all compassionate.

"What the hell is all the screaming about?" he asked harshly.

He stepped over me to go to the bathroom. He was not concerned or at all interested in helping me. Short of breath, I begged him to phone Mama. My mobile home was only about 200 yards from Mama's house.

"Please, Charles, please, before I lay here and die. Please, Charles. Help me, Charles, the baby…Charles?" I begged.

He continued to the bathroom leaving me on the floor unable to move. I knew I had to reach the phone or my baby, or both of us, would not make it. The pain, the bleeding, the fear. I had to get to the phone. Finally, the last digit of Mama's number was dialed.

"Please answer, oh God, please let her answer. Hurry, Mama."

"Hello?" Mama's voice answered, winded. It was like a lifeline for me.

"Mama, please, help me, Mama! My baby, I am losing my baby."

The phone clicked, the dial tone repeating over and over as I let the stretched-out receiver drop to the floor. With Mama living within walking distance, only 200 yards away, I knew help was on the way. Just as Charles re-entered the den where I lay on the floor bleeding, the knock upon the door sounded. He looked at me with fury in his eyes. The knock was louder and louder.

"Sandra! It's your Mama and Daddy!" Mama called anxiously from the outside.

"What have you done, Sandra?" Charles blurted out.

"It's my Mama," I said. "I need help. I am going to bleed to death."

I tried to move toward the door but was too weak. He had no choice but to open the door. He was not about to let me out of his sight not knowing if I would talk about his abuse of me that had occurred earlier. He knew that, once again, he was the reason for all my pain and now another life-threatening situation. As he opened the door Mama and Daddy rushed in. Charles acted as if he was the doting, caring, loving, concerned husband.

"I was lying down and heard Sandra scream for help," Charles told my parents. "I rushed in here from the bedroom. That is when we called you."

Kneeling beside me rubbing my head he was so good at acting and staging the scene. A quality he had obviously inherited from the Queen. The upset husband and father-to-be could not have been more accommodating.

"We have got to get her to the hospital," he insisted.

The nearest hospital was thirty minutes away. The bleeding had been profuse now for about forty-five minutes. I was weak, pale, scared and still shaking uncontrollably. I could not raise myself up off the floor. Mama panicked, and Daddy was pacing. Charles picked me up, carried me to the car and placed me in the back seat.

He whispered in my ear, "This is not my fault. You cannot do anything right."

"Where is my Mama?" I asked in a weakened voice.

"I'm right here. Don't worry, Baby, I'm right here," Mama said with a shaky voice. She had gathered some of my belongings knowing that I would be at the hospital for several days, if I lived at all.

"Please, Mama, ride with me." I was so frightened of what Charles might do. "Please," I begged.

"We will be okay," he said to my Mama. "You don't have to come."

"No. Mama, please ride with me. Mama, please," I wept.

Of course, my Mama wanted to go with me, and she was going with me no matter how insistent he was that she not come with us. When enroute to the nearest hospital, which was thirty minutes away, he took the longest route he could. Then there was a train stopped on the tracks, so the car was stopped.

"Why did you stop?" I questioned terrified, not able to raise myself up to see. My pain was increasing and the bleeding gushing like a waterfall.

Weaker and weaker I grew, a memory of my last trip to the hospital was still fresh in my mind. I had lost my will to live. This was it. I didn't want to live like this anymore. I wanted my baby, but that was just not going to happen now.

On arriving at the hospital, I was immediately admitted and scheduled for surgery. The nurses once again rushed around my bedside inserting an IV for fluids to try and sustain my blood pressure, which at this point was barely palpable. They had to stop the bleeding quickly or the baby and I would both die. So weak, so battered mentally and physically, I had no fight left in me it seemed.

I awakened several hours later with Mama standing over me holding my hand. Her smiling face was so welcomed. Daddy stood on the other side of my bed. I loved them so much.

"Where is Charles?" I whispered.

"He stepped out for a few minutes," my Mama explained.

"Good."

I could not hurt my Mama and Daddy. They were so proud of me for marrying such a loving, caring young man. He was their hero. The one that had saved their daughter's life. Or at least this was what they believed to be true. I just could not bring myself to tell them the real truth. To tell my parents how frightened I was of the cruel, abusive, unpredictable person that I did not even know at times. Charles was always so kind, loving and perfect in the presence of others, but when we were alone it was as if another personality emerged. It was at these times another behind the scenes act of the continuous play, in which he was always the main character, was revealed. I had survived another narrow escape, but I was devastated by the news that I had indeed lost my baby.

"No, my baby! My baby! Why? Why? I needed my baby," I wept uncontrollably.

"Your placenta had detached from the wall of the uterus for some reason," The doctor explained. "Causing your baby to not get enough oxygen and causing you to bleed profusely...I am so sorry."

Emotions overwhelmed me. Bitterness, hate, fear, anger, rage, all surfaced at different times, as I lay quietly depressed, crying, with nothing to say. I knew the reason, Charles. What would he do to me now? I fearfully pondered the future. I despised him. He had been very vocal when we were alone.

"You cannot even have a child right. You can't do anything right. This is costing me days from work. No! No!" he immediately recanted. "I am not going to stay here with you; I'm going to work," he harshly whispered.

Little did he know, but I was relieved to hear that. I wanted to grieve for my child alone. He didn't seem to even care that he had just lost his first-born son. Mama stayed by my side the entire time I was in the hospital. She had told me that if I needed to talk, she was right there for me.

"I just need you not to leave me. Please, just stay with me."

Mama did not push the issue, but she knew there was an underlying uneasiness that I was dealing with.

Eighteen

It was a slow process for me to recuperate emotionally from the abuse before the wedding. And now the abuse that I felt had caused me to lose the most important thing in my life was even more difficult to get beyond. Deep down in my heart I blamed Charles, but only within myself, never voicing it to anyone. I could never let him know I had such feelings. I learned to conceal not only my tears, but my true feelings as well. I would never let him know how I truly felt, not ever again. I would not even try. I had to find a way. I needed to escape.

Oh, God, help me find a way out, was my constant prayer. I dove back into my studying and nurses training. Eager to finish nursing school, even though it was difficult, I felt maybe it was my way out. I needed to support myself to be able to get away from Charles. Needing to get as far away from him as I could possibly get and constantly meditating on a plan to do just that.

Three months later it happened. I had completed nursing school. It was my graduation day. June of 1976 was my chance. My parents were ecstatic, especially my Daddy. I was the only one of their four children to complete college. He was so proud of his "baby girl." But to Charles, it was nothing. He very nonchalantly delayed my arrival to graduation until the last minute. He did not allow me to go early to mingle with my classmates before the commencement began. He was very condescending with his remarks throughout the ceremony, telling me repeatedly that he knew more about nursing than I would ever dream of knowing. He said I was not smart enough to be a good nurse. I had heard these lines many times before, but I concealed the hurt very well and was determined that this day would be mine. Even though he would not permit me to attend the reception with all the other nursing students after the commemoration, I was just glad to have my degree. I was a registered nurse, despite the attempts from him to derail me. I had made it. I had really made it. The planning would now begin. I held my diploma close to my chest and silently prayed. Oh, God, help me find a way out!

Just a few months earlier I had taken a job at the county hospital where I had been treated now, not once but twice. I worked as a nurse aide's assistant on the different medical floors throughout the hospital. Charles seemed to resent me, drilling me like a drill sergeant, asking inappropriate questions about who I had cared for that day at work. How many male patients I had taken care of. What had they said? Did I enjoy it? And on and on he sounded so jealous, so disgustingly perverse. He asked inappropriate questions with sexual connotation as if I was cheating on him. He had to be in control of my every move. This occurred with every shift I worked. Finally, he insisted that I apply for a different job, one not caring for adult males.

"And I mean tomorrow, do you understand me?" he frankly cautioned me.

"Yes," I responded with the only answer I could give.

It was only a week or so after I had applied for the nursery position that I was informed that I would begin my next shift in the neonatal intensive care nursery. This unknowing to him was where I had dreamed of working while in training. Several of my nursing friends had also been accepted to work there. It was the greatest silver-lining opportunity that could have happened. Even though Charles thought he was the one who had made me apply to this area to get me away from the male patients, I never let him know that this was my dream job. I would play Charles' and the Queen's games as I prepared for the grand finale. The workplace became a place of refuge for me. I found peace and a sense of self-worth there. Quickly gaining the respect of the doctors and nurses that I worked with, I began building influential relationships that could benefit me in my plan for escape. At home, the atmosphere remained one of dictatorship. I was no more than a thing, an object owned by Charles. He had succeeded in rendering me defenseless. The abuse, the rape and the loss of my child had all taken its toll on me, for now anyway. I learned quickly not to discuss any part of my work with him, certainly not the fact that I indeed loved working in the nursery and had made so many friends. He would bring me to work and then pick me up at the end of my shift. I had to schedule my schedule around his which was often difficult. If he could not transport me to work, then he would insist that the Queen take me and pick me up. This was just another way of controlling me and limiting my freedom. His mother enjoyed interfering as she continued to control him, and he didn't even see it. I so often felt like a prisoner. Wondering how and why this had happened to me. Why had I allowed it to be this way? As my mind drifted back to the night before my wedding, I knew then that I was making the biggest mistake of my life. However, I had no idea that I would come so close to losing my life, not once but twice. And I lived in anticipated danger continuously.

Our relationship was not a loving one. How could it be one of love? How could I love someone who had abused me, raped me, and made me lose my only child? How could I ever love him? I would never love him again! He temporarily played the role of a caring husband, meaning he would back off the abuse and make promises to treat me better. All the while, he laughed as though this boosted his ego to be so deceitful. I knew better than to fall for this act of the play. Then without any warning he would switch back to the controlling, deceiving, manipulative, cruel Charles that he really was. When the act of love making did occur between us I knew to lay very still and endure. I feared if I moved the wrong way I would bleed to death. He did not know what love was. So, how could he express it? He was harsh, cold and almost inhuman. He could not show any affection as if that would interfere with his role in the play that he was performing in. He did not care about pleasing anyone but himself. And he certainly did not care how painful that act was as long as he was satisfied. Once he was through, he was up and on his way. There was never any foreplay before or cuddling afterwards. It was like changing a tire of an old beat-up truck. There were no emotions involved at all.

"You do not deserve my time to satisfy you."

He would often choose to masturbate in front of me as punishment for things I never knew I'd done wrong.

"Masturbation is better and more satisfying than you are," he said. "There is not enough about you to keep a marriage together." That evil grin always smeared across his face.

Even though I took this to heart as a woman, I blamed him. He had instilled such a fear of death in me that I really did not care if he ever touched me again. I could never have an orgasm with such a brutal animal mentality as he exhibited, when he tried to make what he called love. He had taken one thing from me that I could never replace—my first-born child. He had done things to me that I would never forget. Things that should never be done to another human being. I had absolutely no respect for the demented person that called himself my husband. At this point, I did not care what opinion of me he entertained. Nothing he could say to me would ever matter now.

The next few months I devoted my energy to the second shift neonatal intensive care unit. I was eager to learn everything I needed to know about becoming the best nurse in the unit that I could possibly be. I tried hard to keep things at home on an even keel. Even though I was allowed to drive myself back and forth to work now, Charles would check the mileage on the car frequently to make sure I was not detouring from the route he had mapped out for me. He had the mileage down pat and I would pay for any deviation. He was usually asleep when I arrived home and then he was up and gone by six o'clock each morning. So, time spent with him was less than before and I cherished my time alone. I kept quiet, was very attentive and obeyed him, trying to survive until I could make a way out.

Nineteen

It was four months after the loss of my baby, August 1976, when the test came back. I had been nauseated every morning after Charles left for work. Deep down in my heart I knew. He would not use any protection and he would savagely attack me whenever the notion hit him. The doctors would not let me take birth control at this point after having lost my first baby just four months ago. They had expressed to me that it would be extremely hard for me to ever conceive again. I would probably never be able to have children. I was devastated when they told me this news. I had always dreamed of having children and being a loving mom. Was this because of what Charles had done to me on that stormy night not so long ago? Was it because something had happened to me when I lost my first child? Either way, Charles was a part of the reason. There was no doubt about it, I felt certain it was his fault.

It was positive. The pregnancy test had come back positive. How could this be, so soon after losing the baby? The doctors had said this would not happen, probably never. Oh, my God, what was Charles going to say? How would he react? Would he abuse me again and cause me to lose this child? No, I will not tell him yet. I was panicked. I will figure out what to do,

I rationalized. I kept the news from him for several days. I realized that I should have been overwhelmed with joy of this news. I had wanted my first baby so much. And now, God had given me another chance, one that the doctors had told me would probably never happen. Instead, my joy was negated by the instilled fear of Charles and his reaction to the news.

It was Sunday. We were both off from work. It was a ritual every Sunday that Mama cooked the family dinner and all four children and their families came together to share a meal. Often out of town family would come also because Mama could cook like no one else. After dinner, everyone was sitting around the living room as was the normal routine. I proudly stood before them all.

"I have some news to tell y'all," I excitedly announced.

The look on Charles' face, well, it was indescribable. It was like a scolding look that a parent gives a child just before they are about to mess up.

"I am pregnant," I finally expelled the words.

I felt this was the safest way of telling Charles even though I realized I would catch hell for it later. I felt that this way maybe he would not abuse me again. I wanted the entire family to know, so if he did do something to me, maybe they would figure it out. Mama was the first one up to give me a hug. Daddy was smiles from ear to ear. They remembered how badly I had wanted my first baby. How badly I needed my first baby. Charles just sat there. He showed no response at all. Fearful, I delayed going home as my mind flashed back to the night and place where he had abused me to the point of losing my first child.

The time had come for us to go home. We both had to work the next day. It was just a couple hundred yards from Mama's farmhouse to our home. Not a word was spoken between us on the way. I went straight to the bathroom when we got there. He was watching TV when I entered the living room from the bathroom down the hall. As I stood before him, I was scared. My heartbeat accelerated and my breathing became shallow. He gave me a once allover look and did not say a word. I trembled, my legs weakened, uncertainty was looming heavily. He then grinned his inappropriate grin and chuckled.

"I hope you can at least do this one right, but I doubt you will."

I turned and went into the bedroom. I prayed that he would just leave me alone and not abuse me again. After losing my first baby and being told that I would probably never have children, I had become very attached to a puppy that I had received from my aunt. Muffet was his name. He was an outside puppy, just a mixed mutt. But I had grown to love him and took exceptionally good care of him. I would spend time playing, loving and grooming him when Charles was not around. It seemed that the puppy understood the sadness that lived within my heart and every word that I said. I talked to him very often about my feelings and shared things with him that I could not share with anyone else. Muffet was such a cute ball of fur and so playful. He returned the love that I gave to him. Grandmama would often join us and she grew to love him, too. Muffet brought happiness to me and made me laugh, even through my weariness.

Twenty

Charles was on his way to pick me up from work. He was running late, for whatever reason. I was never to question him about anything, especially his whereabouts. I waited patiently in front of the hospital. I watched him pull into the turning lane behind another car that was turning into the hospital as well. Then suddenly, I couldn't believe my eyes. Another car came crashing into the back of Charles' truck.

The first day I started work as a registered nurse, he had gone back to Tennessee and purchased a brand-new truck. He never shared with me his intentions of purchasing a truck that I would be expected to help make payments on. The car slammed into him so hard that it knocked Charles' truck up on the car in front of him. The driver of the car that had hit Charles got out and ran. I dropped all my work bags and ran from the hospital entrance to the roadway where the accident had occurred. I immediately opened the driver's side door.

"Charles, are you okay? Are you hurt?" the nurse in me took over.

He was a little shaken up, but he proceeded to get out of the truck. After the police came and filed the report, and the truck was towed away, the Queen was instantly there to drive us home. I wasn't exactly sure how she knew to come. But it seemed she just magically appeared at the most unexpected times. It was like she had someone following us reporting our every move to her. The truck was totaled, so we had no choice but to ride home with her. She obsessed all the way home with the fact that Charles did not yet have insurance on the vehicle. I sat idle with nothing at all to say. The Queen was in charge once again. She loved controlling Charles in any circumstance she could insert herself into. She planted seed after evil seed whenever the occasion arose that allowed her to do so. He had no interest in trying to find out if the guy who hit him had insurance to pay for the truck. He refused very abruptly to talk about it. Once home, he went to bed without another word to me.

The Queen went to the police station the next day to pick up the accident report. The police had found and arrested the young man that had hit Charles. But according to the report, he had no insurance. She pursued an investigation into who this guy was and found out that he did have insurance coverage through the owner of the car that he was driving. She also found out that Charles had thirty days to insure a new vehicle. In the meantime, he was covered under his previous car insurance. He was irritated that his mother had taken the initiative to get the situation straightened out. She treated him as if he were not capable of taking care of his own business. Their arguing resulted in the exchange of obscenities and hurtful words. When he and his mother had fights that infuriated him, it was as if the anger ran all the way through him deep into his DNA. He would then turn to me as his confidant. Another game he played very well. It was as if he wanted no part of being around any law enforcement establishment for any reason. This sent red flags up for me as I thought back over the years to the night at the ancient mill, when I overheard the two mill workers talking about his narking and how he got his job with the local power company. What was he hiding that he would pay for a truck that was totaled in an accident just because he didn't want to be seen around the police officers? This was just another hidden mystery.

Twenty-One

Several months into the pregnancy, Charles made me quit my job. It was like he was ashamed for people to see me pregnant. He demanded that I remain inside the mobile home until he returned from work each day. And just so I would not try to go anywhere, he would take my car keys with him to work. He wore me down with his constant emotional verbal bashings. Being pregnant with the hormonal changes and the fear that constantly lived inside me, I began to question the things that he so carefully crafted to beat my self-esteem to a pulp. Maybe I did deserve his abuse, after all I couldn't stand for him to touch me. I did lose the baby. Maybe I did not understand how he felt and why. Maybe things were the way they were because of me. He could see he was wearing me down each day when he arrived home from work. I was almost to the point of total surrender. He felt victorious even though he had not completely won the fight yet. The stage was set, and the arena was all lit up in his mind. He just laughed and laughed out loud.

One day when he came in late from work, I was sitting on the sofa waiting for him. Supper was cooked and ready. The television was playing.

As he entered through the front door without hesitation, he accusingly shouted.

"No wife of mine is going to sit around all day and watch soap operas. All you do is sit around getting bigger and bigger, watching this crap all day."

He immediately walked over to the TV, pulled it out from the wall, took out his knife from his pocket and cut the plug off the brand-new television. I just held my breath. Never saying a word, I prayed silently as I cried without tears. Lord, let him put that knife away. Lord, please protect my baby, please. Memories flashed through my mind of the abuse that had occurred resulting in the loss of my first child. He then turned and placed the knife back in his pocket and headed to the kitchen for dinner. Silence was heard throughout the entire meal. He finished eating then went outside for a little while. I cleared the table and cleaned the kitchen. Crying my silent tears, I was terrified. I had done nothing wrong. I never knew what triggered his outrages that seemed to be more and more frequent.

I always got up with Charles and fixed him a hot breakfast before he left for work. Normally, if he spoke at all before he left, he would make some condescending remark trying to upset my day. He was a pro at knowing how to pull my chain to make me worry all day long. He loved playing his mind-controlling games even when he wasn't here. He left an evil ambience that lingered over me continuously.

As soon as he pulled out of the driveway and I had cleaned the kitchen, I would head next door to Grandmama's. She had gathered a lot of different fabrics and materials for making baby blankets and baby clothes. Grandmama had made most of my school clothes as I was growing up. And she had taught me how to sew when I was in my teens. We would spend the day together talking about the future with the baby and making all kinds of cute blankets and items for the baby. We would often take long walks through the woods of the farm, just the two of us and Muffet, of course. I was safe during these times but I watched the clock very closely as to be home before Charles knew I had been out walking. I was not to leave my mobile home without his permission. I tried adjusting the best I could without verbally expressing my resentment of him for having made me quit my job.

Then it became even more difficult, when he forbade me to go outside or anywhere. He wanted to keep me confined to our mobile home. I felt as though I was a prisoner of war. Never knowing when the enemy would invade and destroy me for good. The fear I lived in was indescribable, but even at that I could not share it with another living soul. I was all alone. He seemed to obsess with anything that made me happy. So, I tried very hard not to show extreme emotion over anything while around him. I had learned to cry without tears to hide my emotions and more importantly I had learned to hide the truth.

It was early morning, the birds were chirping, the sky was bright blue, the pastures were rolling in a plush green carpet of grass. Charles had gone to work. After I had completed my daily chores as usual, I eagerly was on my way next door to Grandmama's. But something was strange. Muffet was always right there waiting for me the minute I opened the door. I stepped outside, closing the door behind me, but he was nowhere to be found. I rushed into Grandmama's mobile home just a few feet away from mine.

"Muffet is not here. Where could he be? He never leaves me," I said.

I was beside myself and on the verge of tears. Grandmama and I hunted for hours, in the woods, down the road, and over to the neighbors. He was nowhere to be found. He had just vanished. It seemed to me that everything I loved went away. Day in and day out I would call Muffet from the back door. He never came. He would have never left me on his own. I knew he loved me; I knew it. For weeks, I did not go out of the house. Charles had only laughed at me with his inappropriate grin stretched across his face when I mentioned to him that Muffet was gone.

"Even the dog doesn't consider you worth being around," he boasted.

I began to doubt my self-worth as a human being. I was depressed over losing my child, quitting my job, and now the puppy I sought refuge in was gone. Muffet was the only one I could express my deep innermost feelings too and live. I lived in a hell-hole prison box; a 12- foot by 65-foot torture chamber, with an insane drill sergeant. If he spoke at all to me, it was only negative, manipulative and condemning words. I had to use my imagination of happy times as a means to survive. Happy times with my Grandmama, my family, and Muffet because there had never been any happy times with Charles. Ever. From the very beginning of our relationship, he would not even call me by my name. Instead, he would refer to me as an animal, mostly a pig. He seemed to relish in the expression that I wore as I heard the sardonic words as they came from his malicious mouth. How could I have been so blind as to not see his depraved personality under that smooth facade that he displayed for everyone else?

Twenty-Two

It was a very sultry, still day. I was anxiously awaiting the delivery of my baby soon. I had gained a lot of weight just in the mid-section. The baby had been estimated to weigh around nine pounds. I was slow in getting up and down because the baby had moved into a low position getting ready to be born. I was inside when Charles demanded that I come out and sit in the car to mash the brake as he bled the air from the new brake shoes he had placed on the car. He had been outside most of the morning replacing the brake shoes that had worn down. I was always grateful when he was tied up doing something else and I was not in his path of his destructive behavior.

I did as I was instructed. As I entered the car I accidentally hit the horn, and it sounded loudly. Charles came from around the front of the car, his face full of vicious anger, his fingers clenched so tight that his knuckles were white. He suddenly jumped into the air and kicked the windshield of the car, breaking it into a million pieces. I sat dazed, frozen in time for a moment.

"It was an accident. I'm so sorry. I did not mean to do it, I'm sorry," I repeated over and over.

I sat there with my head in my hands, hiding my tears once again. I could not fathom how much more I could stand. Please, Lord, help me. Help me find a way out before he kills me. Unbeknownst to me, Grandmama had been watching from her kitchen window and had witnessed the whole event.

The very next day when Charles had for sure gone to work, Grandmama came to visit me.

"Sandra, there will come a day that you will be glad to see him go down the road and never come back," she said. "And if you want to know what happened to Muffet, just look in the trunk of his car and you will find the answer."

She told me these things as she held me close with her arm around my shoulder. Nausea swept over me like a wave at high tide. I felt so sick at the thought of him killing an innocent animal that I loved so much. Just what was he capable of? Would he hurt me next?

"Please promise me you will never let Charles know," I pleaded with Grandmama in a panicked, trembling voice. "Promise me, please, that he will never know that you and I know the truth."

I was frightened that if he found out that Grandmama had been watching him, he might try to do something to her. I could not risk the woman that I adored getting hurt because of me. I knew that he was capable of anything. Even to this day, he does not know that I knew he killed my Muffet. Just because I loved Muffet, he killed him. I knew if he was aware I had found out the answer to the Muffet mystery, he would strive to hurt me some other way. He would take something else, or someone else, I loved away from me. No, I could never let him know. I knew deep down that my Muffet loved me and that he did not just up and leave me. I knew he would have never left me, I thought fearfully to myself. How could he be so jealous of an animal? I tried not to show too much affection to

Muffet when Charles was around, but I never mistreated Muffet. He was my confidant and best friend, the only one who really knew the hell I endured daily.

It was three weeks past my due date. I was admitted to the hospital on April 28 for an induction to help deliver my baby. I labored long and hard. I was apprehensive of how Charles would act and what he might say in front of the people I had previously worked with. Would he belittle me as though I was a mere animal giving birth to his child? Or as just a used-up vessel to house his offspring? Would he show any affection toward me or my baby? I was panic stricken with the fear lurching over me from my past. What if the baby being born tore the weaken area in the vagina where Charles had ripped me so close to death before? Would I bleed to death before they figured it out. The doctor delivering the baby was not the same doctor that had helped save my life before. These doctors did not know what had happened to me back then. I was afraid to share with them about the abuse I had endured at the hands of Charles. It was a secret I could tell no one, even as it now put my life in danger once again, after all this time.

Fourteen hours passed, and I had not made any progress at all in delivering the baby. I was so tired, weak, pale and exhausted. My condition was deteriorating.

"We must do a Caesarean Section immediately or we will stand a chance of losing the baby and the mother," the physician explained to Charles. "The baby is just too big to be born vaginally."

Charles was beyond livid.

"You can't do anything without screwing it up," he said belligerently. "Why could you not just have this baby the right way? I knew you would not do it the normal way. I am tired of waiting."

He had no compassion at all for what I was going through, or the thought that we might lose our baby. He did not care that I was weak, scared and so filled with terror for my baby. He was asked to step out for a moment while the nurses prepped me for immediate surgery. I was relieved that he had been dismissed. I had rather be alone to deal with all my emotions with just me and God, without Charles' evil presence. I was prepped and ready for surgery quickly. As the nurses wheeled me upstairs to surgery, my angry husband was nowhere to be found. My Mama, Daddy, and Grandmama were there as always to support me when I needed them. The nurses wheeled me by my family waiting in the hall and paused while Mama and Daddy leaned in to give me a kiss.

"We will be right here waiting and praying for you and the baby. Grandmama is here too," Mama said.

"I love you, Sandra," Grandmama said as she reached for my hand and gave a big squeeze. They were all so excited and a little concerned at the same time as I was headed once again for surgery. If only I could tell my parents the truth. But I could not. Not now. Probably not ever.

On my way to surgery, I was relieved in a way. At least the baby would not be coming down the vaginal canal and I could stop worrying about being torn apart and bleeding to near-death like before. Oh, Lord, thank you. I know you are watching over me and my baby, I prayed silently.

Twenty-Three

I woke to my Mama, Daddy and Grandmama standing over me with extreme happiness radiating from their faces. Mama could hardly wait to speak.

"You have a beautiful nine-pound, twelve-ounce baby boy, and you are going to be fine. He is so beautiful," she said.

Everyone was talking in a state of excitement and relief.

"When can I see him?" I asked anxiously. "I want to hold him."

Charles was not there. Where was he? Did I really want to know? I did not ask. My concern was my new baby boy. He would be my sole focus now.

Then the dark-haired woman who stood five-feet nine-inches entered my room. She was athletically built, not fat, but hefty. It was Charles' mother, the Queen.

"He's beautiful," she cheerfully expressed, like everything was great. My mind flashed back to the last time she had entered the hospital room that I was admitted too. Nothing in my world was great with the exception that now I had delivered my newborn baby and I had found the strength to work on my plan of escape. Mama and Daddy excused themselves to go back to the nursery to ask how much longer it would be before I could see my baby. Grandmama stepped out with them.

"Where is Charles?" I asked his mother.

"Oh, he is out there at the nursery window all hugged up with some slutty looking girl named Allison. I told him he ought not to be acting that way with you all laid up in here after just having surgery," she said with the same inappropriate grin that I had seen on Charles' face hundreds of times.

Unable to hardly move, much less think about getting up, all I could do was wait. It was not until the nursery nurse brought little Alex to me that Charles came into the room. He had very little to say. It was more than obvious that he was still upset with me about not being able to deliver the baby on my own. But that was okay with me, because I was so spellbound by my little man, Alex. I examined every inch of him. He was so perfect and absolutely gorgeous. He became, at that very moment, my reason for living and the added strength I needed to complete my mission.

Charles did not stay at the hospital. He left, I assumed, with the slutty girl that the Queen had mentioned. Were they working together, Charles and the Queen, to destroy the most wonderful day of my life? I now had a beautiful healthy baby boy and that was my focus. I suddenly had a reason to survive, no matter what schemes they devised. He was my someone I could love, and he would love me back. Mama and Daddy were so proud of me and the baby. Of course, Grandmama was proud of me, too. But Grandmama conveyed a strong sense of concern that only I understood. No one else picked up on it but me. Grandmama and I had that kind of a relationship.

I named him Alexander because it was such a distinguished name. He was the most beautiful child I had ever seen. He had jet black hair, deep dark eyes, and his skin glowed. He was perfect. There had never been such joy in my life before and now I had strength, such strength that I thought

I could make it through anything. The strength I needed to find a way out for me and my baby.

After seven long days in the hospital recuperating from having a caesarean section, I was released to go home. Charles had been in and out to visit us during the seven-day stay, but he never stayed very long on any of his visits. He remained very cold and distant toward me. He denied that what his mother had said about the slutty girl was true. He swore the Queen was crazy, as he sat there with the famous inappropriate grin plastered across his face. The Queen had also visited several times throughout the seven days. I felt like it was to stay abreast of everything that I did or said. This way she could stay in control, manipulate and cause trouble. This was her role as the leading lady of the Black's play. She paraded around as if to admire her own performance.

Mama and Daddy had to work, but if they had known I was uneasy and frightened to have this woman alone in my room with me, they would have never allowed her to be there. I would endure until I could get on my feet and make my plan of escape.

Charles had always threatened that there was no need to try to tell anyone about our relationship behind closed doors, because they would never believe me. He told me I would never be able to hide from him.

"I'll always find you no matter where you try to go," he said. "It would just be a matter of time." He laughed aloud with such a wicked sound.

Grandmama was waiting at my small mobile home when I arrived with baby Alex. She was elated with her arms held wide open to receive and welcome her grandchild and great-grandchild home.

"He is radiant," she said proudly. "He is an angel."

I felt secure for the first time in a long time. The baby was here, and I didn't have to worry anymore about Charles abusing me to the point of losing another child. I was beyond that now. My loving parents and

Grandmama being around gave me a sense of security. I worked hard to recuperate after my surgery with little help from Charles. I was focused on a renewed life with a strength that I had never known before. It was a supernatural strength. I knew how close my Mama was to God and how she prayed for me daily. I often felt like my Mama had an insight to unknown things that were going on like Grandmama, but never voiced it as not to interfere. But she certainly charged angels around me and I was well aware of them.

As for Charles, he remained the same abusive, cold-hearted son of Satan that he had always been. Having a child made no difference in him whatsoever. He was a Black and there was no changing him. I decided to go back to work as part of my plan. I convinced Charles to agree to it, because it would help us financially. He gave in right away when he considered the money side of it. He was a greedy and cold self-centered character that certainly was the leading man in his mother's play. I knew I needed finances to be able to secure a way out for me and my baby. I was trying extremely hard to make the best out of a horrible situation for me and baby Alex. Oftentimes, I felt sorry for Charles. He was so dysfunctional, because he had never experienced love, the real love of a family. Even now, he could not see what a blessing God had given him in his very own child. I was rehired in the neonatal unit of the same medical center where I had almost lost my life. I worked hard at becoming an excellent nurse. I also worked hard to build a skilled professional relationship with the five pediatricians that I worked closely with. I loved my job. It was at times hard for me to function at my expertise level, because Charles would often deliberately assault and abuse me just before I left for work. I would also worry about my baby at home with Grandmama. What if he tried to take him and leave? She would certainly put-up a strong fight to keep that from happening, but what if she got hurt in the process? I was only able to withstand a lot of what he shoveled upon me, because I held on to the concealed fact that I would have a plan as soon as possible to escape this living hell of torture. A plan that would save me and baby Alex. If he ever tried to take or hurt my baby, that would be the breaking point. That thought was never far from my mind. I had slowly developed a stronger personality after giving birth. I now had a natural instinct of protection for my child. Whatever it took I would protect him. I had to make sure as soon as possible I could produce a plan that would not fail. Charles was capable of anything. No one in my family had ever seen the evil that consumed him behind closed doors, but I had lived in its presence.

I gained more confidence as a nurse, despite the condescending remarks and opinions of my darling husband. With my precious little Alex to protect, I grew stronger within myself. After some time, it became easier for me to let the words of evil personified roll off my shoulders. I focused more on my reason to live, baby Alex. I knew I must play my part in the Black's day-to-day theatrical production, with the star, the Queen and her leading man, her son, Charles. I always knew that there was a very deeply hidden underlying exchange between him and his mother, one that triggered a wave of uncontrollable storms that raged within him from time to time. I had sensed it from that very first encounter with his mother. The Queen never approved of any relationship that he had ever been in. She claimed him as her own property. I did not know just how dysfunctional this whole group called the Black family really was until much later. Even though she did not approve of him marrying me, she had accepted it, because she did not want him to go to jail for rape. She was going to see to it that would never happen, even if she had to destroy me at any cost. The two had parallel personalities. Just any little thing could trigger her deepest depraved evilness to appear in a flash. Charles was the best one to bring this about in her. My memory flashed back to her kitchen table before we were married.

"You would be a fool to marry Charles," she said. "He is evil and obsessed. He has a personality dysfunction that runs on his father's side of the family. Mr. Black is a mental case, too. His mother passed it to Charles, and he will pass it to your children if you marry him."

I quivered all over as though an artic wind passed by me. I could see Satan himself through the dark eyes of his mother. How could a mother say such awful things about her own son? I wept for Charles. Am I the only person who has ever cared about him? It was at these times that I gave into my affectionate side as I was such a soft-hearted young woman. I had compassion for everyone, especially children. That was just part of who I was and the nurse in me. But now, after all this time, I had experienced firsthand the dysfunction of the entire family. It was horrific. All I knew was I wanted out and I wanted my child not to be subjected to the Black's dramatic performances. I realized that just being around and having been captured and woven into this web of evil, I was changing in order to escape. I prayed never to become like any one of them. But I had to toughen up and learn how to meet them head on.

Twenty-Four

I played my role in the Black's play, gaining perfection as time passed. Trying to keep things quite on the home front, I was determined to stay out of Charles' range so as not to provoke him in any way. However, at times, there was a rage and a fury that would just erupt from him, deep down from within and I never even knew the source from which it came.

I loved my job and was secretly gaining influential friends that could help protect me and my baby down the road. I worked patiently on a plan of escape. I knew it had to be one of precision, no errors. I had to have everything well thought out, because not only was it my life now, but little Alex was in the equation, also. Charles remained the leading man as the play of the Black's saga continued, and he was in charge of my entire world. At least he thought he was, but he could not control my thoughts. I had mastered how to conceal my true emotions and the despicable dislike for my husband that grew greater with each passing day. He was still very demanding, using sex as punishment for something I said or did not say or something I did or didn't do. I could only guess which one. I never had the opportunity to enjoy the act of what was supposed to be making love with someone who shared feelings of true love. Instead, I was subjected to an animal instinct and evil satisfaction of accomplishing a victory in the arena of the bedroom. It was like he was performing before the Queen for her approval. How sick could a person be? But he was just that—sick. I always wondered if he would hurt me again like the first time. Each time he mounted me, I reverted to that stormy night because his demeanor had never changed. He was always there for the kill, performing for the ones that were living out the play they themselves created.

I continued with my daily routine of work and caring for Alex, and of course, accommodating Charles' every whim. Mrs. Black, the Queen, continued to play her role quite well. She was constantly planting evil seeds in Charles' mind about how I did not measure up to her expectations of a wife or a mother. If he spoke to me without being arrogant or cruel in front of her, she would then say something about his childhood that would immediately trigger an outrage. He would hit the wall, throw things and cuss. The Queen would just laugh. She, too, seemed to relish in causing hurt and destruction whenever she could. She demanded all the attention and the spotlight so to speak to always be placed on her as the leading lady, the star, the Queen. He had shared very little about his past or childhood with me, but he often shared bits and pieces when he was overcome by anger at his mother. This anger was beyond the typical anger that a person would on occasion exhibit. This anger was evidence of severe abuse and hurt from many years of endurance. Maybe, as far back to a very early childhood experience. Even at that, he would strive for her approval in all he did as though trying to make up for years of failure.

He once shared that, up until the time he and I wed, his mother would come into the bathroom and sit with no clothes on and watch him shower. Being taken back by this I asked.

"Why didn't you lock the door?"

"I did, but she would use a nail she had hidden to get in," he said defensively.

I cringed at the thought that Mrs. Black had probably molested Charles at an early age. The mysterious family that lived on the secluded hill had more hidden secrets than I could have ever imagined. He was defenseless against his mother. Even though he talked back to her as though he despised her, she was always able to win control of his thinking. She had an invisible hold over him that even he did not realize. She voiced her opinion about every aspect of my life. She dictated to Charles step by step how he and I should live. What he should buy or not buy. How I should decorate our home. She continued endlessly. She tried to convince me that I was not a good mother to my new baby boy. The Queen was always very vivid about her opinion that I was a very weak, uneducated and homely girl. I had maintained a B average throughout my nursing training, but that was just not good enough. Mrs. Black's role in this play was to continually encourage and entice Charles to do things to hurt me. Her relationship with him was beyond strange. It was as if she was a scorned woman who had lost the affection of her son to another woman. She was so jealous of me and her goal was to destroy my marriage anyway she could and to take the one thing that mattered to me—little Alex. I had never and would never again encounter a group of people that called themselves a family that would behave like these people. Never a kind word was heard in their household. They were always cussing, fighting, and saying evil things to each other and speaking negatively about everything. If I could imagine what Satan's household would be like, that would be it. The Queen would re-enforce her declaration of how Charles had different personalities and how he was not normal, every time she could isolate me. As I listened to her, I realized that it was this evil woman that had made him so different. What all had she done to him? No wonder he could not speak of his childhood and would escape with bouts of destructive rage at the mention of it. Often the fury and rage from him would explode from just a glimpse from her. A volcanic reaction would occur within him as a memory from his childhood would be sparked. He often spoke to me of his hate for his mother. Yet he seemed to strive to please her and only her as though he were a little child seeking for approval that was never fulfilled. I never shared my opinion or thoughts as I listened attentively whenever he would be so overcome with anger at his mother that he released a few of his innermost hurts. Then as though he had never let his guard down to share, he would meander around the house like an emperor in his palace. He was very demanding and always issuing orders as if he had to prove and exalt himself by threatening me into submission of his every whim. I could never share with him all the negative, disgusting statements and suggestions that the Queen shared about him whenever she could manage to be alone with me. Suggestions that would plant seeds of doubt in my mind about his sanity and our marriage to the point of making me want to leave. She knew the whole time that I was trapped and could not go anywhere. This was just another torture strategy that she blatantly exhibited.

I always got up before Charles and prepared his breakfast and lunch before he left for work. But this morning he rushed around and refused to eat the breakfast that he always requested I fix for him. He would be leaving a little early with no explanation as to why. He could have shared that with me before I had gotten up and prepared breakfast. It was as though he thoroughly enjoyed the inconvenience he caused me. As he was leaving, he made a demeaning remark about how I could not do anything right. With the sound of the car cranking and backing out of the drive I felt a great sense of relief. I rushed into the bedroom where Alex was sleeping soundly. I sat and watched him sleeping and prayed that God would soon reveal a way out for me and little Alex. As I sat in the silence, I remembered the Queens last conversation with me. The topic was Charles stopping at a store on his way to work to have breakfast with several women there.

"You must be mistaken," I said. "I always cook breakfast for Charles."

"No, I spoke with the owner of the store myself," Mrs. Black adamantly stated. "She shared that she has a daughter that is very attracted to Charles, but everyone in the community knows she is just a slut. Charles supposedly really loves her homemade biscuits. Don't be too surprised if Charles decides to stay with me for a few days."

It was obvious that the Queen was playing her leading role again letting me know that she knew more about what Charles was doing than his own wife did. Supper was on the table waiting for Charles' arrival from work. I was pacing because the food was getting cold. He would be coming in and go into one of his raging fits if the food was the least bit cold. Or so I thought. He was late, an hour, two hours, then four hours. Not a word. Then the phone rang.

"Hello?" I answered.

"Sandra, I thought I would let you know that Charles will be staying a few days with me. He is outside shooting his guns right now, but I thought I'd let you know."

The Queen's voice was so elated, almost like she was singing her favorite song. It was more than obvious to me that she had orchestrated this a few days ago.

"Okay, thanks for letting me know," I said calmly, then I hung up the phone.

I lived in misery for the next three days. The misery of not knowing when he would show up again and in what kind of mood. He always seemed more abusive and malicious after being around the Queen. I dreaded the day and time. The not knowing.

I was feeding Alex when he opened the front door. He came in as though he had never been gone. I knew not to ask any questions. It was late. Without a word after being gone three days, Charles went to bed. I rocked the baby until I could hear the snoring from the bedroom. I sat on the sofa frozen with fear. Afraid of making a sound that would awaken him. I finally fell asleep from exhaustion.

"Wake up! Are you going to fix my breakfast?"

His raised voice startled me as he shook me. I wanted to say go eat with your friends, but I knew better. Without saying a word, I got up and fixed his breakfast, he ate and then left for work. Once again, I held Alex tightly and prayed. Oh, Lord, please protect my baby. Please, Lord, help me keep him safe. Please take these evil thoughts of me poisoning Charles or disabling him so he can't hurt us. Please, Lord, take them from me. I don't want to be like these people in thoughts or actions. Help me, Lord, please.

The mind torturing games played by both the Queen and Charles were enough to push anyone to the edge. It was as if they were working as a team to destroy me completely, little by little. I always knew the slightest little thing could trigger him into a rage. Therefore, I had to walk on eggshells to protect me and my child. I could do it for as long as it took.

One day when he came home from work, he told me to sit down. He had talked to his mother and had decided that he and I needed to build a bigger house. She and Charles had been looking for land. So, he now wanted to include me in looking, too. Stunned, I thought to myself without showing any signs, what is the Queen up to now? She had just a few days ago demonstrated how easily she could persuade him to her way of thinking without him even knowing it. Why was he telling me this now? I really had no say so in the matter at all.

On his next off day, he insisted that we go with his mom riding around to look at property. I left Alex with Grandmama and went along with them. It was a disaster. The Queen was definitely in charge. She and Charles rode in the front seat and I in the back seat. Letting my imagination run free, I was trying to come up with a plan of escape from such an evil den of dysfunctional people. Then the car stopped, bringing me back to reality. She had brought us to a dilapidated old rock house. I knew not to say a word. She immediately began telling Charles how he could make this house livable. He would not have to spend much money at all, she cheerfully continued. She was not at all unaware that this was bothering me tremendously as she recommended all the improvements she would make on the house. This was not at all what I had in mind. It was at least a hundred-year-old rock house that smelled ancient. No way would I want to live there. I had discussed the house plans I had with Charles back before we were engaged. Before he had shown all his true colors. He had completely agreed that would be the house we would build when the time came. The plan was to live in the mobile home and save our money to build our own home, not buy a house of the Queen's choosing. I had reservations now after all that had happened to me. I would never feel safe moving away from my safety zone of help. I needed them to be close by in case I needed their help again, like before. When we returned home, I remained quiet. I knew it would not matter what I said anyway. But inside, I felt the urgency more than ever to find a way out.

It was early one Saturday morning when he informed me that we would be going to an auction of some land nearby, not very far from where we lived now. He had not shared anything about this land with me and certainly not that he was thinking of buying it. I again left Alex with Grandmama as Charles and I went to the auction. I was so surprised when the Queen did not show up. She and Charles had had a disagreement, a big disagreement. He never said what it was about, and I did not ask. But I knew it was big for her to miss this opportunity to direct the next act of our lives in her play. I had never been to an auction before, but Charles bought twenty-eight acres with the money we both had saved. I was not sure what this was all about. Did he do it to aggravate the Queen? Was it a trick to intimidate me? He always had an alternative motive for everything he did. After the auction we went straight home. He sat me down and said he wanted our lives together to be different. He would treat me better and build me the house I wanted. He was very convincing. What personality was this? Without a doubt it was one I had not met previously. I had been down this path before—a crooked path built with broken promises. I remained silent, never letting my focus wander away from little Alex and my plan to escape. Never forgetting the things Charles had done to me. Nothing could ever make up for the things he had taken from me. Did he really think I was this naïve to fall for such lies? I totally despised him at this point. All I wanted was out, away from these evil dysfunctional people and to protect my little Alex.

A week or so went by and the phone rang.

"Hi, this is Mr. Johnson with the auction company preparing the deed for the property Charles purchased."

"Yes, this is his wife, Mrs. Sandra Black."

"I just needed to know if the deed should be put in both your names."

"Yes, of course," I said with an expression of unbelief on my face. "Absolutely."

I started to tremble inside. Charles was at work, and I would never speak of that phone call. I prayed he would never find out what Mr. Johnson had asked me. I knew what would happen if he did. I was never considered in any decisions to be made. He always told me I was not smart enough to get out of the rain without him. He would not even allow me to vote. Mr.

Control, himself. I was constantly contemplating a plan of escape. One that he could not control! But I felt God was watching over me and little Alex. Maybe this was a part of the plan for our escape.

Several months passed. Charles had contacted a builder and the foundation of my dream house was poured. He had been a little more relaxed with no communication from the Queen. Even so, I was not about to let my guard down. This was the man who had raped me, manipulated me and cost me so much to the point of almost losing my life, twice.

Then it happened. The Queen reappeared, center stage, in a state of emergency, almost. Performing with a sense of urgency, as though she had to catch up and gain the momentum she had lost in her absence. And that she did. Charles returned right away to the stage of the Queens' play. I was very aware of the performance unveiling in front of my eyes. She wanted him to abandon the plans for the house and build one open room with one bathroom. He listened very tentatively. He then turned to face her and seemed to agree with her, ignoring me completely. Once again, the Queen had sabotaged my life. Destroying any hope of my dream house being built was now her next act. I remained incredibly quiet as I listened to him cower down to her. I waited until he and I were home to attempt to speak to him about the house. I trembled with fear as I expressed to him I had rather continue living where we were until we could build the house that we agreed we wanted, not the house she wanted. I had not ever voiced my opinion like that, but I was so tired of the Queen entering, raising and closing the curtain as she wished. He responded by looking at me as though to look straight through me. He never acknowledged that I had even spoken to him. I had definitively changed. The battle had begun, and I had stood for once.

Twenty-Five

The foundation of my dream house stood for over a year, the backbone for a structure with no weight to support. Work on the new house had ceased. The Queen lavished in her accomplishment of the script she had written in her mind. She had re-entered for another act in the Black's play with only destruction in mind. She decided now to attack me using a totally different avenue. She was planting seeds in Charles' mind about me keeping Alex from her. She insisted that he let her keep Alex while he and I went to a movie. I could see right through this kind, loving act of hers.

I said no, but Charles quickly reminded me that he was in control. I did not want the Queen keeping Alex for fear of her influence or what she might do to him. After all, what had she done to Charles? Only heaven and the walls of the mystery house knew the answer to that question. How could he trust her now? Was he once again seeking to prove something to her? At the risk of his own son? Before I knew it, she had blown the script up to paint me as such a horrible person for keeping Alex from her.

Without warning, I was confronted by Mr. Black as Charles and I were gathering hay in the field down below the mystery house. Mr. Black hurriedly came down the hill and with tension boiling through his body, he drew back to hit me. He was literally shaking and cussing, knuckles turning white, shouting at the top of his lungs. This was a total extreme behavior that I could have never imagined from such a docile man. It was as if he himself was performing for the Queen as she sat at the window of the mystery house watching.

"You have got Joni (the Queen) crying and so upset!" He expressed in an uncontrollable state. It was the first time Charles had ever protected me, but he stepped in front of Mr. Black, stopping the blow to me.

"What the hell?" Charles yelled excitedly.

He was just as surprised as I was. I stepped back and gasped for breath. I was able to cry without showing my tears. I stood speechless. I could not believe what I was hearing from Mr. Black's mouth. I had not done the things Mr. Black was accusing me of doing. Things the Queen had told him. I was surprised. I had never known Mr. Black to voice anything. He only spoke when spoken too. He had obviously been instructed and programmed to act under the orders of the Queen. Had Charles really stepped in to protect me? Or did he hate Mr. Black, too? He had never had anything nice to say about him and certainly never referred to him as his dad. He hardly ever spoke to him at all. That scene certainly did not go as the Queen anticipated. Charles withdrew from her and began building the house again. He even included me, asking my opinion and what I wanted. But I was suspicious, of course. I knew not to get too comfortable because it was just a matter of time. I was skillful at hiding my feelings and had learned to play my role in this depraved, vicious production.

Alex turned nine months old, and I was still praying every day for God to reveal a plan of escape. Charles' personalities and moods were the same. Though it seemed he had traded around and had chosen to be less intimidating at times. Then, out of nowhere, he would revert back to the leading man on the Queen's staged production.

Twenty-Six

I woke up feeling so nauseated. I had been suspicious, but would not accept the thought. Charles refused to use any protection, and my doctors still would not allow me to take birth control because of the high risk of blood clots.

I held Alex tightly.

"Oh, Alex, this is not good timing," I smiled as I talked to my sweet baby.

God, how will we be able to escape now? Oh, God, why now? I had no way of knowing that pregnancy was all part of God's plan. I had no idea how much I needed this baby to give me added strength and to be a help to Alex. I would come to realize as the plan unfolded. I cried for hours. What would Charles say? What would he do to me? How would I tell him? He was a lot different when distanced from the Queen. But I still walked lightly, never knowing where the edge was.

When he came home from work, I had his supper ready and waiting, as I had always done. I knew not to approach him when he first came in. I had to assess his mood to determine what reaction he might have to the news. Sometimes, just a simple look his way might trigger an outrage. I decided to wait until after the dishes were cleared and Alex was bathed and put down to bed.

He was lying on the sofa watching TV. He had repaired the plug he had cut off in one of his earlier performances. However, I was not allowed to turn the television on, only he could do that.

"May I talk to you, Charles?" I asked for permission.

He sat up as to grant permission. I sat on the other end of the sofa.

"We are going to have another baby," I spoke softly as my heart throbbed in my throat. I trembled inside, not knowing what he would do or how he would react. He was silent for a few moments, as if thinking about his response.

"Well," he started. "I guess we need to rush the building of the house, since we will have an addition to the family."

I was so shocked, but relieved for the moment. Thank you, Jesus, I silently prayed. Lord, I will have two babies now that I need you to protect. I need you more than ever, Lord. Please help me. That became my continuous prayer. I tried extremely hard to keep from upsetting Charles in any way. Of course, that was impossible to do, because he never needed a reason to act out his rage and anger. My focus remained on Alex and now this pregnancy and my plan of escape. Charles still had his bouts of unpredictable performances of control and authority, but I did not allow him to hurt my babies. I was determined to protect Alex and the baby at any cost. Never would I let him take another child from me.

Nine months later, on November 6, I had another C-section and delivered a beautiful blonde-haired, eight-pound six-ounce baby boy. I was so excited that he was healthy, at least I thought he was. He was so beautiful. He was named Noah because he was so special. Little Noah and I had to remain in the hospital for seven days. I had not been away from Alex overnight at all since he was born. What could he be thinking? He was only eighteen months old, not old enough to understand. Grandmama and Mama were taking care of him. The Queen was not able to come around because she had contracted an infection in her hip joint and was bedridden in a body cast.

"We must go by on our way home from the hospital and let her see Noah," Charles said.

So, of course, we did. From day one, the Queen made condescending remarks about how Noah and his blonde hair could not belong to the Black family. She immediately started planting seeds of doubt in Charles' mind, doubts about me and my baby. Never taking an intermission between the acts in her play. Even from a bedridden state, the Queen continued to exert her role on a stage of deceit. She had not been around for a while, but her re-entries to the stage were always filled with intense drama.

Baby Noah turned six weeks old, and it was time for his six-week newborn check-up. I was devastated to learn that Noah had a heart murmur, indicating a hole in his heart. The doctor said he had found it in the nursery when Noah was born. He had hoped it would resolve on its own, but it had not. I knew that I could not share this with Charles. I was afraid he would disown Noah, since the Queen had already decided that Noah was not part of the Black Clan. What would Charles do to me or to my baby? I left the doctor's office in a state of shock. I felt so guilty thinking that I was being punished because of my mixed feelings about being pregnant at the beginning. I did not want to subject another child to the torture and abuse of such a dysfunctional family. I was so afraid. I was trying to escape. I was in a constant state of unrest, overflowing with a tormenting fear of the unknown.

Twenty-Seven

Christmas was right around the corner. Once again, the Queen was in control of what gift Charles would buy me for Christmas. He had told me to write a list of five things for him to choose from that I would like to have. I had done as he requested.

It was a tradition on Christmas Eve that my family would all meet at Mama's and Daddy's with all the children to eat and exchange gifts. Charles was always one to act the loving-hero part in front of the family, and that night would be no exception. The moment arrived—Christmas Eve. All the family gathered around and exchanged gifts, but there was no gift for me.

"Oh, here is one with no name," my brother said. "I'll open it." Inside the box was a door knocker, an ugly door knocker. "What is that?"

"Oh," Charles spoke up. "That's your gift, Sandra."

Fighting back the tears, I looked away. I knew at once that the Queen had struck again. An ugly door knocker was certainly not on my Christmas list. Charles just sat there with the inappropriate smile across his face. I had learned to disguise the hurt from the unexpected surprise attacks quite well. My focus was always on my boys and a plan for a way out. At times like that, it just encouraged me to be more determined than ever to seek refuge as far away from those deranged people as I could possibly get.

The Queen had insisted that little Alex and little Noah not be told about Santa Clause. Christmas was always a big deal around my family and home. It was always a special time filled with joy, laughter, and love. I wanted my boys to experience what I had known growing up at Christmas time. This was just one of the many ideas that the Queen would fight me concerning the boys. It was always going to be a raging war, because she had declared it long before our marriage took place. There was nothing that I could do to make it better. I was just not good enough for the Queen's son. How dare I take him away from her. Little did I know, but she was now planting seeds of doubt about Noah throughout Charles' whole family. She said that Noah belonged to the milkman (a matter of speech meaning someone else) and certainly not to Charles because he had blonde hair. One of her sisters approached me when I was out shopping with my Mama.

"I can understand why Joni (the Queen) says that Noah does not belong to Charles," she stated quite frankly. "He looks nothing like their family." She just turned and walked away. Even the extended family seemed to be rude, cruel, and disgusting. Whatever the Queen spoke was written in stone to them. They all appeared very ignorant to the fact of how a child inherits their physical traits. Wow, I thought to myself, what was that about? Is his family so narrow minded to believe that because a child has a different hair color than the father that it is not his child? This just made me love my child even more, if that was even possible.

Even though I would be exhausted, I stayed awake at night watching Noah sleep to make sure he did not stop breathing. Day in and day out, I was distraught at the possibility. Knowing Mama had a direct line to God when she prayed, I could no longer bear the weight all alone. So, I confided in Mama about Noah's condition. Always so loving, she gave me a huge hug and told me not to worry any more. She then called her prayer warriors together and they prayed for little Noah.

On Noah's next visit to the doctor, the problem no longer existed. Noah was healed. I had my confirmation that God was listening, and he would deliver me and my two boys from this insane arena that I had somehow allowed myself to become entangled in. As Noah grew older, the Queen always made such a difference in the way she treated Alex and Noah. She would say that she could only love Alex, because he belonged to her. He was her grandson, as though Noah did not exist. She remained bedridden for just over a year. Mr. Black waited on her hand and foot. She would talk to him in such a degrading manner, it seemed he could not do anything right either. She would often tell me stories about how mean and awful he was to her when they first were married. She told me that when she gave birth to Charles' youngest brother, Mitch, that Mr. Black would not even come to the hospital and bring them home. It was so ironic that Mitch had blonde hair and Mr. Black had jet black hair. Maybe it was from her own experience that she questioned the light hair color. Still, Charles could not see through the Queen's attack on little Noah because of his blonde hair. She said that Mr. Black always felt that there was something wrong with Charles when he was born because "he looked wimpy." She always spoke very poorly of Mr. Black's family saying that they all had mental issues. She felt that Charles had inherited mental issues from them. A concept that she repeatedly expressed over and over again. I was still in the process of learning, but had a pretty good idea of how the Queen maneuvered her attacks of manipulation based on her thought process of deception. It was very hard for me to comprehend the Queen's way of thinking, since I was in no way evil or deceptive. But I studied her, and I was learning. I hoped to beat her at her own game someday. She had no idea what I really wanted. She may be very surprised to find out.

Twenty-Eight

Charles continued to build the house and things were okay as long as I concentrated on my children and did not rock the boat. I put forth extra effort to stay out of his line of fire. There was very little contact with the Queen during the first year of building the house of my dreams. There were times when I thought that maybe, just maybe, he was beginning to become a different person. I still walked around on eggshells in the things I said and did. Still extremely fearful and refusing to let down my wall. I had a tiny safe place in an imaginary corner of my world. It was as though I was out of sight on the stage of the Queen's play just waiting for the drastic change to occur without any warning. I often sat dazed thinking of the things that had occurred around me, not really knowing how in the world I got there. It was a place I did not want to be and certainly did not want my children to be. Oh, God, protect us. Please, God, help me find a way out.

I was pulling the night shift at the local hospital in the neonatal intensive care unit. It was a stressful job to say the least, nevertheless, one that I truly loved. I would work all night then take Alex, age two, and Noah, age one, to the building site of our new home. I would clean up where the contractors had worked, then install insulation in the walls until time to cook dinner for Charles. I rushed home to cook and have dinner waiting on the table every evening when he arrived home. After cleaning the dishes, I would try to sleep three or four hours before going to work. He was supposed to bathe the boys (which only happened if he wanted to) and put them to bed. I would kiss them good night on my way out and pray to God to keep them safe. I was so exhausted, many nights crying all the way to work praying over and over for God to help me find a way out for me and my boys. What had I ever done to deserve a life of consuming fear, constant pretense, pretending to be happy, yet totally devastated underneath it all? I was determined to search to the bitter end for a way out that would give me peace and protection for my boys.

I could not believe the house was finally completed. Charles took me to pick out furniture. He even let me choose the décor I wanted. I was very conservative. I did not want to push my luck and upset him to the point of changing his mind. The next day the furniture was delivered while he was at work. I worked hard to get things in order enough for us to move in. Two days later, we moved into our new home. I should have been ecstatic, but so many mixed feelings lingered—fear, anger, anxiety and confusion. I had been tricked before. It was such an uneasy feeling, a feeling of gloom and uncertainty hanging over me all the time. I was paralyzed by not knowing when the evil that was always lurking overhead would swoop down and turn my world upside down again. I hated living this way. All in God's timing. I know, Lord, you will hear me and give me a way out, I prayed. I was concerned now with two children and a house that it would not be easy to escape. Charles was taking my paycheck from me before I could cash it. He had to approve every dime I spent. That had always been a rule I had to live by from the beginning, which made it extremely hard for me to put back any money for me to use to escape with the boys.

Two weeks had passed since we moved into the new house. I did love the furniture and the house I had dreamed about for so long. However, as I sat there, I realized that it was not at all the home of which I had dreamed. It was just a house. The dream of a loving, caring husband, of laughter and joy as the children played, seemed to have faded. The feeling of overwhelming delight to come home to someone waiting and enjoying their company over dinner and playing with the children; it was just not there. I had to pin up all my feelings. I was just an object to Charles. There was nothing to look forward to when he came home. In reality, I dreaded the thought of him walking through the door every evening.

The doorbell rang. Who could that be? As I opened the door, the two men who had recently delivered my furniture were back to retrieve it.

"We are sorry ma'am, but your husband phoned and said he was not pleased with the furniture and wanted it returned today."

I was in shock and so embarrassed. Why had Charles done this? No doubt, the Queen was back on stage and in the shadows. When he came home, I had his dinner ready and waiting. He went upstairs and immediately came down. He opened the back door cursing and threw everything I had cooked out on the carport.

"What are you doing?" he yelled. "Trying to kill me with this crap you cook?"

It was the same meal that he had so often requested. This was the second time he had accused me of trying to kill him with what I cooked. He then immediately got into his car and drove off. As I watched him leaving down the long driveway, I was so confused. It all happened so suddenly, as though he just needed an excuse to justify his leaving. It was not the leaving part that I was worried about, but the part when he returned was my concern. I stood amazed. Killing him was sounding more and more like a good idea.

Welcome back, Queen, the stage is set and ready for your grand entrance.

I always knew without a doubt when Charles had communicated with the Queen. He always seemed to punish me as a substitute for what he wished he could do to her. Physically, emotionally, mentally it was a toss-up as to which method he would choose. But I always knew when the curtain lifted and the Queen was performing, I would be the one to suffer. I cleaned the kitchen, then fixed me and the boys something to eat. Then I bathed the boys, read a bedtime story and gave them a big hug and kiss, and put them to bed. He returned hours later. I was ready for bed, not saying anything upon his entry. I just rose from the sofa in the playroom and went to the bedroom praying that he would not hurt me. I lay on the edge of the bed on my side with my eyes closed as though he could not see me if I kept my eyes shut. I laid perfectly still, almost not breathing. He came to bed but never said a word to me. I was not able to sleep for fear he would do something to me or the boys in the middle of the night.

He woke early the next morning. I had already gotten up to fix his breakfast and lunch. I could hardly wait for him to leave for work. Without saying anything to me, he was gone. I breathed a sigh of relief, then went into the great room and sat in the middle of the floor of the empty room and cried. I had the furniture I really wanted. I just couldn't understand why he had done this. After all, I worked a full-time job and was contributing to pay for it. I went over and over in my mind what I might have done or said to trigger him to send the furniture back. Did he take it back because he thought it brought joy to me because I liked it? I had tried not to convey my feelings of really liking it. Whatever the reason was, it did not take long for him to convert back to the leading man role in the Queen's saga. Charles and the Queen were working hard to wear me down in such a way that I would break, but little did they know that I had found even more strength to fight now that I had both my boys. My reason for living had doubled. I would survive. I had to succeed for them. I sat and held my babies so tightly, making them a promise that I would protect them forever. We would escape together. Little Alex and little Noah were too young to understand that they were the only reason I was able to endure. God knew that they would need each other, and I would need the two of them to be able to continue. Now I understood God's timing with the pregnancy. Little Alex and little Noah were only eighteen months apart in age. They were like twins that with a special bond to care for each other.

The doorbell rang. I opened the door only to greet the two men that had retrieved my furniture the day before. They were now bringing it back.

"What?" I was so embarrassed again.

I was friends with the daughter-in-law of the owner of the furniture store. I also worked with the wife of one of the delivery men. I knew that it would be rumored at the hospital where I worked that my husband had done this. I should have been elated, but instead, I was nauseated. The men brought the furniture in and arranged it where I had it placed before. As I was thanking them, the phone rang.

"Hello," I answered hesitantly.

"Did they bring the furniture back?" Charles asked.

"Yes."

How did he know they were there with the furniture? Did he have cameras installed to know who was at the house? He seemed to enjoy displaying the criminal leader role. Instilling an increased sense of fear and questions in my mind. I knew not to ask any questions, but I just could not understand. He had seemed to have been better for the past ten months, not having any communication with the Queen. Then abruptly, he started his unpredictable, dysfunctional behavior all over again.

A couple of weeks passed, and the furniture incident was never discussed. That's how it was around there. If it was not talked about, it had not happened. I focused on loving my boys and working. I always kept my eyes on my focus of developing a plan, a way out.

It was a bright sunny day, and I was about my normal routine of taking care of the boys and my chores around the house. Charles was at work, and I always felt a little reprieve during those hours. I felt like there was always an aura of evil hovering over me. I never knew what to expect, so I always kept my guard up. The continuous production of the Queen's play was never ending.

The doorbell rang. I was almost afraid to answer, and for good reason. Believe it or not, there stood the two men from the furniture store once more. As tears welled up in my eyes and no words spoken, one of the men stepped inside and gave me hug.

"I am so sorry," he said.

Without any further conversation they took the furniture away once again. As they were leaving, I stepped outside and motioned that I needed to tell them something.

"Would you please tell my friend Amber to refuse to deliver it again?" I ask in a low voice. "Just in case he should call."

The tall man that had given me a hug replied, "Yes, I understand."

Once again, I sat and cried for hours holding my two boys. When Charles arrived home, I had his supper ready and on the table. He went upstairs, then came down and ate without a word. He was never very playful with the boys, having very little if anything to say to them. Often in his moments of rage he would threaten me by saying that he would take them from me, and his mother would raise them. He was good at taking away or trying to destroy anything that I loved or cared about. I knew that he meant what he said, even more reason for me to find a way out. I did my best to keep my distance and not rock the boat.

Several weeks later, he came home late from work. He and the Queen had another disagreement. She had called him at work and asked him to come by her house on his way home. He did not share what the argument was about, but he threw a letter down on the table from the Queen to me. In the letter the Queen stated her intentions of taking my boys. She stated that I was not capable of being a good mother and labeled me an unfit mother. The letter said that I was afraid that Alex would love her more than he loved me and that he had said he wished I was dead. Alex was just three years of age, and the word dead was not in his vocabulary. He was such a happy, affectionate little boy, and he loved his mama. That was for certain. The letter continued with unfounded accusations against me. I became extremely nauseated as I continued to read. I did not dare dream of discussing this with Charles. For all I knew he could have helped to write it. Why would he even present it to me if he had not been a part of it? I just kept silent and retreated to the bathroom to gather my thoughts and pray. I poured my heart out to God. Please, God, I cannot take much more. Please help me protect my babies. Please get us out of here safely. Please, God? I wept. What would I have to do to stop the evil Queen? It did not matter; I would do whatever it took. She would not ever take my boys from me. Whatever it took.

Twenty-Nine

As I continued to read the letter from the Queen that Charles had given to me, it went on and on with nothing but negative accusations about me and baby Noah. When I finished reading it, I was shaking inside and sick to my stomach. No one had ever spoken to or about me in such a degrading, cruel, unsubstantiated way. Once again, the Queen had succeeded in being able to plant seeds of distrust and doubt into Charles about me, and now Noah. She was quite a character in the play that she continuously acted in. She paraded around the stage with the inappropriate smile across her face as though she were light years above any of us.

The Queen was eventually up and out of the bed and on a walking cane. Charles and I had completed the house and moved in while she was out of commission, but now she was back. She told him how ashamed he should be that he had treated her in such a way and that I was the cause behind it all. As usual, after a few days he was right back at center stage, starring as the main character in the great saga that the Queen continued to direct. Without even informing me, he had invited the Queen and Mr. Black to come for a visit. He instructed me that's how it would be.

"If you plan any function at the house, the Queen is to be included. Birthday parties for the boys, family gatherings, Christmas parties, etc. the Queen will be invited. Understood?"

Charles opened the door just as the doorbell rang. In walked the Queen and Mr. Black. The stage was already set, the curtain rose and the Queen in all her glory with the smirk of an inappropriate smile walked across it like the Queen of Sheba.

"Well, Sandra, looks like you have no furniture," she said sarcastically. As if she did not know about the furniture incident. The smirky smile revealed she knew very well about the furniture. After all, she was the director of Charles' every move.

"You know that picture is hung way too high," she criticized. "Don't you know that it should be at eye level."

I chose to remain silent. I was cordial, but behind the pleasant façade, I was praying for a way out. The atmosphere of the looming evil was so heavy and thick that I excused myself so that I could catch my breath. After a couple of hours, the grand tour and all the condescending and patronizing comments had been made, they departed. Never during the visit did either the Queen or Mr. Black speak to Noah; only to Alex. I noticed those hurtful intentional omissions, but did not dare mention them to Charles.

A few days after the grand tour, on Charles' day off, he instructed me to get dressed he would be taking me to get the furniture back. I was so embarrassed that I did not care if I ever got any furniture. As usual, the knot in my throat arose and the overwhelming fear was at its height. I did not want to face the people at the store again, but I really did not have a choice. I asked Mama to watch the boys while we went to the furniture store. The disappointment on arrival at the furniture store had me holding back my tears. Most of the furniture I had picked out before, the furniture I really wanted, was already sold. However, no complaining or voicing of disappointment was heard, I simply made other choices. The manager of the store met us as Charles was getting ready to pay for the furniture. The manager explained to him that this sale would be final. It could not be returned. As I turned aside, I saw my friend Amber in the distance, and she gave me a wink. This was a relief for me. At least when the doorbell rang again, it would be for delivery only. I felt like he had only retrieved the furniture to spite the Queen. Their relationship was one of such hatred. It was like a pendulum swinging constantly from one extreme to another. No way to know where the pendulum would land.

The Queen continued in the months to come to interfere at every opportunity possible. She voiced her opinion in every decision that arose in dealing with a new house—from the cookware to the landscaping. She always had to have her say. Charles could never seem to stand on his own against her. In return, he had to exert his locked-up frustration toward the Queen onto me.

I had a night off from the hospital. I had waited to watch a movie advertised on TV for several weeks. I was sitting quietly by myself in the playroom upstairs. The boys were already bathed and put down for bed when Charles came into the playroom. He sat down and asked me what was on the TV.

"It's the movie I wanted to watch."

He immediately got up and turned off the TV. He told me to go to bed.

"But Charles, I just wanted to watch that movie. I'm not sleepy."

I knew I was not allowed to turn on the TV, but I had not expected Charles to come in so soon. He quickly jumped up, pulling me up by one arm and told me not to talk back to him. He pulled me to the top opening of the flight of stairs that led from the upstairs to the downstairs. Pulling my head back with my hair and holding me with a grip around my neck that took my breath, he whispered in my ear.

"I can throw you down these steps and kill you in a way that no one would ever know that I threw you down the stairs. They will think you just fell." He began to laugh as he pushed me through the bedroom door and slammed me onto the bed. "Now do as I tell you!"

I was petrified, frozen with fear. What would be next? Oh, Dear God, help me find a way out. I stayed still on the bed, sobbing silently, shaking uncontrollably. I knew it was just a matter of time before he carried out his threat. He returned to the playroom and continued watching TV until the morning hours. When he came to bed, he snatched me from my side of the bed. He ripped my panties off me and rolled me over on my stomach all in one hasty motion. He then began threatening me again. He pulled my buttocks apart with his bare hands, tearing the skin up my back a good two inches. The pain was unbearable. I screamed loudly. He threatened me to be quite and not wake the boys. He continued to tell me how I was not fit to be a mother or a wife. I could hardly move from the pain radiating up my back. Not sure at this point what he had done to me. I just knew that it hurt intensely. Charles just laughed and let me go pushing me to my side of the bed. He turned his back to me and was snoring in no time. It seemed he gained such pleasure in the demented things he did to me for no reason. I could not move I was so frightened that I would disturb him, and he would hurt me more.

The next morning, I got up not having slept at all and checked on my boys who were sleeping soundly. Just looking at their little innocent bodies gave me strength. They were both so beautiful and my reasons for existing. Barely able to walk, I went downstairs to the kitchen and fixed Charles' breakfast and lunch. He came down, ate, and left without a word. I never sat and ate breakfast with him. He preferred it that way. It was as though I was a servant girl, not worthy of eating at the same table as the royals. It was always such a relief to see him going down the driveway.

I often thought of my Grandmama's words, "There will come a day, Sandra, you will be glad to see him go down the driveway and never come back." Grandmama was always right. That day had come. He had destroyed any love that I might have had for him. Now, my only concern was finding a way out before he killed me.

A few days passed and he remained distant and cold. I continued to try not to rock the boat. I did not want to die. I only responded when spoken to and that was not very often. He made me feel like I was not capable of carrying on an intelligent conversation with him. In his way of thinking, he far outranked me in every field. That was okay with me. At this point in my life, I just wanted out.

The next night he came into the bedroom when I was getting ready for bed. Once again without warning he threw me face down on the bed. I began to beg.

"Please, Charles, what have I done? Please don't hurt me again,". The more I begged, the more he laughed.

He then pulled my head back off the bed with my hair and put a gun to my head. "You will do as I say. I will have a list of ten things that you are to do before I will ever have sex with you again."

"Okay, Charles, I will do anything for you," I said, hiding my tears.

He laughed as he released me. I slid off the bed to the floor knowing better than to let him hear me crying. He seemed to be aroused whenever he hurt me to the point of surrender. I was still healing from the tearing of my skin up my back that he had brutally inflicted on me a few days prior to this.

The next day he walked in from work and presented me with a list of the ten things I was to do. As if keeping sex from me was a punishment. Little did he know that was more than fine with me. He was like a barbaric, insane human. I was at the point where just thinking of his touch was grotesque to me. I associated his arousal with horrific pain, in every sense of the word. How was I ever going to escape? The list presented to me included:

1. You are to always walk behind me.

2. You must ask permission before buying anything, even if it cost a dime.

3. You will wear only the clothes that I approve.

4. You will keep the house immaculate.

5. You are never to go anywhere except the route I designate.

6. You are not allowed to watch TV.

7. You must lose weight.

8. You will not talk on the phone.

9. You are not allowed to have anyone visit when I'm not here.

10. You will never ask questions about anything pertaining to my whereabouts.

I was so sure that the Queen had a hand in this, but I was not interested in having sex with Charles anyway. So, that list was not a big deal to me. It just made me work harder and pray harder for a perfect way out for me and my boys. I had shared cautiously with an attorney friend, a scenario that I said was a nurse I had met at the hospital in an abusive marriage. My attorney friend told me she knew of a case that the woman was so badly abused that she waited until the husband was asleep and shot him. She got off. Not that she was advising that someone should do that.

"I am just saying your friend doesn't have to live like that."

She told me about another case where the wife set her husband's bed on fire and he died.

"Abuse is real," she said. "Send her to me and I will try to help."

"I don't know if she will come," I uttered quickly. "She is so afraid, not just for herself, but her family as well. I am not completely sure of what she is dealing with. I'm not sure I will tell her I've talked to you."

Over the next few days, I rehashed the conversation with the attorney as I went through my daily routine. I thought about how relieved I would be not to worry about Charles hurting my boys. Could I go so far as to kill him? I shook my head. What in the world? What kind of person was I becoming even thinking such thoughts? They were destroying my character. This was not me, thinking this way. After all, my mission and purpose in life had always been to help people. And what about my boys? There had to be another way. Charles was in my head again. No, I will not let him win. He will not destroy me and my family. I will not stoop to his level of evil. I will find a way out. I could not believe I had entertained those kinds of thoughts, even for a brief moment. I quivered inside and out and asked the Lord to forgive me and for strength to do the right thing and to help me find a way out.

Thirty

I was cleaning in the downstairs great room. Charles came in and walked right over to me and as I turned, I caught my breath. He had startled me. He spoke bluntly.

"You and the boys have been holding me back in what I want to do in life. I am going to Saudi Arabia to live and work."

I was taken aback, not exactly sure what he was saying.

"Are you taking us with you?"

"No!" Charles shouted. "I just said you are holding me back."

"Oh, okay, that's fine. What about the house and the payments? I cannot make it and take care of the boys on my check alone."

"I will send money home for the house payment."

Thoughts were racing through my mind. Oh, thank you, Lord, it's my way out.

"Okay, Charles, I will wait a year for you to go and figure out what you want. When you come back, and I do not want this anymore, you will have to agree to let me and my boys go."

He became irate. Fury was a mask he wore well.

"Oh, hell no! If I can't have you, no one will. I will burn this house down with you in it before I let you go. You belong to me."

"But, Charles," I said in a soft voice. "I thought that is what you wanted, to be free."

He stormed out of the house and did not return until the next morning. He came in and to the upstairs where I was.

"Have you started working on your list yet?"

"Yes," All the while thinking what a sick man. I still wondered if the Queen had written the list for him. There was no mention of the conversation from the evening before. I still believed that God was working a plan for me and my boys to be rescued from this nightmare.

I finally reached the point that I knew for my safety and the safety of the boys, I had to get out.

"Hello, Law offices of Cook and Mason."

"Yes, I need to make an appointment to talk about a divorce," I spoke with a scared trembling voice.

"Can you possibly come tomorrow morning at 10 a.m.?"

"Yes, ma'am, I'll be there."

The next morning, I got the boys to Mama's and was preparing to leave for the appointment with the attorney. Charles was at work. I was backing the car out when my collie, Bella, that I loved so much, was playfully running around and slid under the back wheel of my car. Bella was lodged underneath my car and could not get out. I tried hard to get her out but could not. I frantically called Daddy. He had always come to my aid no matter what he was doing. He never delayed. He worked to free Bella, then drove me and Bella to the vet. While we waited for the vet to check Bella out, I was so distraught.

"Daddy, I was on my way to the attorney to see about a divorce," I confessed. "I did not want to disappoint you and Mama because y'all thought I had a great life."

At least I thought that was what they thought.

"I have known for a while now that you were unhappy," he patted my hand when he spoke with such mercy. "I have noticed that you never smile like you used to. Your Mama and I have talked about it, and we will support you in whatever decision you make." He hugged me like he didn't want to let go.

"I want my baby girl to be happy," he said with teary eyes.

He had no idea that I had lost my true smile and my bubbly personality because of the horrific pain I had endured, the continual threat that lingered over me and the uncertainty of the hidden evil that resided backstage of the Queen's play. There was just no way that I could release those tantalizing memories of the rape and the saga that had been unfolding since. I could not share that with anyone. There was just too much at risk.

The vet came back with news that was not good. Bella had broken her back and there was just no other way but to put her down. I collapsed into Daddy's arms.

"How much more, Daddy? How much more can I take? This is entirely my fault."

Daddy comforted me, holding me in his arms and letting me cry as if I were a little girl again. He put me in the truck, took care of the bill and retrieved Bella's body.

"I will bury Bella where I have buried all the animals that have passed away on the farm."

On the way home, I called the attorney and told him what had happened and rescheduled an appointment for another day. I was so distressed after what had happened with Bella that I was reluctant to try to make it to another appointment to see the attorney. I had lost something that I dearly loved, again. What if Charles found out and tried to take my boys? They were what I loved most and could not live without. They were my reason for making it this far. But I knew I had to do it. My time was running out.

A few days later, I made it to my appointment with the attorney. I had gone incognito, circling around in different directions before finally stopping at his office. I was so afraid that someone might be following me. I knew that if Charles got wind of what I was doing, he would kill me and take my boys. I knew that without a doubt. If he checked my mileage, I would have to account for the deviation in the route he had designated for me. I had to be ready with an accurate explanation just in case.

I was very honest with the attorney and answered all his questions. His advice to me was, "Get out as quickly as you can for your safety and the boys."

As I left the attorney's office that day, I felt sick to my stomach, experiencing severe nausea and stomach cramps. I was so scared and horrified with a sense of urgency, thinking about what would happen to my boys if I died.

About a month later, when I had saved enough money, I proceeded with filing for a divorce. Charles had always demanded that I give him my whole paycheck without cashing it. He would then give me money if he felt I needed it. I managed to save the money he gave me to eat on and from a few other things. Mama and Daddy gave me the rest of the money I needed. The attorney assured me that the papers would be served to Charles at work. I would be notified before that happened, so the boys and I could go somewhere safe.

I was up early as usual. No sign of Charles to be seen. It was his day off from work. He must have left without making a sound, or I was just too exhausted I did not hear him. I was sitting in the playroom folding clothes while Alex and Noah were playing and watching TV. Charles came in and up the stairs to the playroom. He was wearing overalls and had a shotgun on his shoulder. Standing in the doorway, he slowly took the gun from his shoulder and pointed it directly at me. He never said a word.

"No, Charles! Please, Charles, don't do this," I begged. "Don't do this in front of the boys, please."

The boys just sat there staring up at their dad not moving an inch. They sensed the danger. Charles then lowered the gun and began laughing as he walked out of the house. I could hear the backdoor slam. My heartbeat was throbbing in my ears. I immediately grabbed my two boys, ran downstairs, and got in my car. The driveway was a good distance from the house to the main road. Overcome with fear and shaking uncontrollably, I went as fast as I could. As I turned onto the main road I could see Charles walking down the road with the gun on his shoulder.

"Alex, get down in the floorboard and keep Noah down there too," I said sternly.

As I raced passed him, he pointed the shotgun at the car and laughed. I fled to Mama and Daddy's house. Daddy was at the barn and Mama was in the kitchen. I went in with the boys. I was as pale as a ghost and trembling as though I had just seen a dead person. I could hardly catch my breath. I had begun to ask Mama if me and the boys could stay there for the night when Daddy came through the front door. He always made me feel better and safe no matter what the circumstance. I just sat there holding my two boys tightly. As I was telling Mama and Daddy what had happened, the police scanner in the background caught my attention.

"What? That is my address!" I said frantically.

The police scanner was dispatching a fire truck to the location I had just left. I immediately flashed back to Charles saying he would burn the house down with me in it. Had he gotten the divorce papers without me being notified? I asked Mama to watch the boys and I ran out the door to my car. I sped in the direction of my house, which was not far from my parents.

"Sandra, Sandra," Daddy called out as he was beating on the window of my car.

I was crying so hard I never heard him. He finally got my attention. I had pulled off the road just before my driveway. The house fire was directly across the road from my house. I thought that Charles had gotten the divorce papers and had burned our house down, just as he had threatened.

"Sandra, it's okay," Daddy insisted. "Now go back to the house and wait with the boys."

Daddy was a captain on the fire department, and he knew the firemen there. He stayed to talked with them and found out that the house was deliberately set on fire. I felt like Charles was sending a warning to me. He would do what he said he would do, and he would get away with it. No one was ever charged with setting fire to the house across the street from my house.

I went back home the next day. I left my boys with Mama. I feared for my life, but I knew if Charles suspected anything, it would be worse. I had gotten exceptionally good at pretending and playing the role assigned to me in the Queen's play. I would have to continue a little while longer until the divorce papers could be served, and he'd have to leave.

When he came in from work, he seemed different. He never mentioned the gun or the house fire. *What goes through his mind?* I thought as I stared at him without him knowing it.

"Where are the boys?" Charles asked.

"Oh, Mama wanted to spend some time with them. I thought it would be okay."

Trying very hard not to trigger him in any way, I looked down at the floor as I spoke. As long as Charles thought he could cower me down he was happy.

Thirty-One

Charles was served with the divorce papers at work a few days later. I had informed my attorney of the gun incident and the housefire across the street. He immediately put a rush on getting the divorce papers served.

"I am very concerned for the safety of you and your boys," he said with genuine concern. "Please stay alert to your surroundings. Be very careful and use caution until we can get this resolved."

I was at home without the boys when Charles came home from work. He had been served. He seemed very happy. He came in and got a few of his things. He turned to me as he was leaving.

"I'll tell you one thing; I don't want you, but I won't let anyone else have you either."

Out the door he went. Exactly what did that statement mean? I pondered, but did not speak a word. I stood behind the curtain of the side window watching as he backed out and went down the drive very slowly. I was sure he would head straight for the Queen's palace. My heartbeat raced with relief and fear all at the same time.

At least I knew my boys were safe with my Mama and Daddy. I could hardly stop the cold tremors. I was overcome with the repulsive feeling of what was to come. I knew the Queen all too well to know that this was not the end, but a continuation of the saga that will be full of tabulated tortuous scenes directed by the Queen. Does Charles even realize how he is being cloned by her? Even to the point of non-existence, except when he steps onto the stage of her great play. I thought to myself, how sad. I could imagine the great Queen smiling and twirling around, scheming to write the next scene which would focus only on destroying me and capturing my boys at any cost. I gathered my thoughts back to the present reality and rushed over to Mama's to check on my boys. As I arrived and turned into the long driveway that led to the farmhouse, unexpected memories flashed across my mind, remembrances of that night long ago, the pain as fresh as if it were just yesterday. I immediately stopped the car and burst into tears, sobbing hysterically as I relived the torture of that night that Charles had brutally raped me and almost caused me to lose my life. It was as if God was reminding me that it was time to do what I had finally resolved was the only way I could live to raise my boys. I had really tried to be a good wife at the beginning, trying to convince myself that everything was somehow my fault. That I was supposed to be able to love Charles enough to help him heal and change. At this point, I knew that it was just too late to sever the cord from the Queen. She was like the master of a permanent puppet show. She could pull his strings from even great distances away and control his every thought.

I pulled myself together enough to continue to the farmhouse where my boys were. I was so glad to see their smiling little faces as they came running out to meet me. I always greeted them with a big hug and kiss. My Mama and Daddy also came out to meet me. They would never understand how much they meant to me and how much I needed them.

Later that evening, I lay with my boys in my bed and held them as close as I could get them to me. I was totally exhausted, physically and mentally, but there was no way I was going to close my eyes. A state of being that would grow to be a consistent normal for me; with an overwhelming fear that lingered and hovered over me at all times night and day, no matter where I might be.

The boys and I remained at Mama and Daddy's house over the next week. I wanted to give Charles time to get his things and move to the Queen's house. The insurmountable fear of evil lurking around every corner followed me every minute of every day. I not only had to worry about what might be brewing in his mind as far as revenge, but also what the Queen may be preparing behind the next curtain in her ongoing production. My main concern was the safety of Alex and little Noah. They were my reason for living and no one was going to take them from me. I had grown a resilience to stand as a mama bear would to protect her cubs. I knew that I had confirmation from God in what I needed to do. And now there was no stopping me.

A few days later, he drove up unannounced at the house and wanted to talk to me about the divorce. I was hoping he was sincere in trying to remain civil concerning the division of property and the visitation with the boys. He sat and talked to me in a way he never had before. I had not seen this side of Charles ever, not even when we first met. He left that day in complete agreement that we would remain civil for the boys. I stood amazed. He had never been concerned about the boys. I knew that he had rehearsed with the Queen to try to throw me off my guard. I was not at all sure and could not even try to imagine what the Queen had in mind for the next act of her play. One thing I was certain of, it would not be good.

The hearing date for the divorce was set. The attorneys had drawn up the divorce decree and I had agreed to what I discussed with Charles, but obviously the Queen had arrived on the stage again and Charles was not happy with the agreement that he had proposed. I shivered as I sat on the cold pew outside the waiting my turn. I had never been in a court setting before. My doctor friends had instructed me on what attire I should wear, the colors that were permissible in the courtroom and how to address the judge with my answers. I was very naïve in matters involving the court. I had never dealt with attorneys or judges before.

Charles and I had sat down and discussed what he would take and what he would allow me to have from our thirty-one hundred square foot house. The house and twenty-eight acres would be sold, the bills would be paid, and the equity would be divided equally.

When it was my turn to be heard, I was called to the stand immediately. As the attorney for Charles began, he questioned me about my finances and financial reports stating that I had taken money from a doctor that I worked with, insinuating that I was selling favors. Totally blindsided, I knew this was absolutely from the Queen. Even though the accusations were completely false, an evil seed was planted once more. Finally, the judge made a ruling for Charles to pay $525 dollars every month. Charles was not in agreement. The Judge ordered that visitation would be every other weekend. Charles worked at the local power plant and made a good salary, but the judge ruled for the attorney fees to be paid individually. I was barely making ends meet as it was. Charles refused to pay his child support, and it seemed the court would not do anything to correct him.

Charles made sure that the divorce was delayed for a year, and since Christmas was my favorite time of the year, he had my signed divorce papers delivered to me at Christmas. This was just another terrible gift that the Queen and Charles had chosen for my Christmas gift.

He was granted visitation by the judge. However, he would send the Queen to pick up the boys, and he would be gone on a trip with his new girlfriend, whom he had begun seeing long before the divorce was ever filed.

Several months before I had filed for a divorce, he had purchased a spitfire sport car without me knowing. He made it clear that I wasn't allowed to drive it. Only a few days after he purchased the car, he left without telling me anything of his plans. All my family went to Florida every year in early July. Charles and I, and the boys always went with them. It was time to go, and he had not returned. No phone call or anything. I really thought that since we had already paid, he would come back home to go. At that time, I did not know of the many affairs he had been having or who it was that was with him. I still had not heard a word from him. I had no idea where he had gone. I had taken the time off from work, so I took the boys and went on to Florida with my family. While there, I phoned him several times but got no answer. Me and the boys returned home at the end of the week and still no sign that he had come home.

When he did come home, nothing was ever said about where he had been or with whom he had been. This was the summer before I had filed for a divorce, and I only learned much later of the several affairs that Charles had prior to me filing for the divorce.

I was concerned when the Queen would pick up the boys, because she was so vengeful and downright mean to Noah. She always made such a difference in the way she treated the boys. She would do things that she knew was contrary to what I would approve of for the boys. She taught them to throw rocks at passing cars and bought Chinese stars and other dangerous things for them to play with. She said awful things about me in front of them. She called me on the phone and told me lies about my family just to upset me. She viciously went around the neighborhood spreading the same lies, trying to destroy me and my family; just like she had told me she would do years ago. She told my Mama's friends that Charles was the perfect husband and couldn't understand why his marriage went wrong. She said Noah did not belong to him.

Satan is a liar, I reminded myself.

The Queen was clearly enjoying her trophy winning performance of contentious behavior against me. I begged the court to limit visitation to be supervised and requested that Charles had to stay with the boys. But, of course, Charles and the Queen would continue to play the stage their way. He refused to pay his child support, so I had to take another job to make ends meet. She always composed scenes for her play that were arranged to cause me discomfort. I was to oversee selling the house because me and the boys were living there, but the Queen would take real estate agents there and go all through my house while I was at work without notifying me. She removed several things from the house claiming they belonged to Charles, because her family had given them as gifts at the wedding shower. She took paintings off the walls, figurines from the curio cabinet, books etc. She paraded around as though she lived there. She thought she had the right to do anything she chose to do. When I realized what the Queen was doing, I immediately called one of my friends that had authority, and he in return contacted the realtors and they threatened to sue her. I had decided to stand up to her. I would stand my ground with her, even though I knew that it would be all out war when I did. I had already listed the house with a realtor that a doctor friend had recommended. The real estate market in the area was moving very slowly. Charles phoned me and threatened to proposition the court to auction the house off immediately. I begged for a little more time. He just hung up the phone. At the sound of the dial tone, I stood there with the receiver clutched in my hand, thinking. The Queen is performing again.

I had enough dealings with the court to know that Charles and his aunt who worked at the courthouse had enough pull to get the judge to agree with whatever he wanted. His aunt had enough favors, or threats some would say, to get the judges and attorneys to act in favor of Charles and what he wanted no matter what it was, especially all the married ones that she had slept with.

Within the next two weeks I received a phone call from the realtor. He had a prospect that was very interested in the house. He was moving from out of state to manage a well-known company in the area. He wanted to meet with me to tour the house without the realtor. I hesitated, and silently drew a deep breath. I found the request very strange, but with all the pressure from Charles about auctioning off the house, I agreed to meet with him. We scheduled a time to meet on my next day off from work and then hung up.

I had been so battered for the past eight years that I trusted no one. I was so tired, a kind of tired that sleep cannot fix; an emotional tired that ran deep. I meditated on the reasoning behind this man wanting to meet with me alone. Somewhere deep inside I felt the Queen was somehow behind the meeting.

Two days later, I had taken the boys to Mama's so I could meet with the potential buyer. I did not worry about the condition of the house, because I always kept it immaculate. I sat on the large front porch that expanded the width of the house waiting for the man's arrival. As I sat waiting, I allowed my mind to wonder back in time. It was as though I was suspended somewhere between then and now. I remembered all the abuse, the rape, the loss of my child and finally the grand finale of getting my dream house just to have it taken away. I had emerged into such deep thought of the cruel spoken words, the threats of confinement—both physical and emotional—that I suddenly realized all the silent tears I had held back were now streaming down my cheeks uncontrollably. I had learned so many years ago to cry without tears but now that I was alone, it no longer mattered.

I wiped the tears away with both hands. I resurfaced to reality as I saw a car coming up the long winding circular drive. A tall, slender, attractive man emerged from the vehicle. He looked to be a few years older than me. I stood to greet him at the top of the steps. He introduced himself as John and the tour began.

The house was very impressive, as his remarks revealed. As he made his way through every room, I felt very uneasy. I still pondered why he wanted to meet with me alone. Was this a set-up? Was the Queen playing me once more? Had she indeed sent him so she could accuse me of wrongdoing to use against me to try and take the boys?

Mr. John was very personable and seemed concerned that I was selling such a beautiful home. I was overly cautious with this stranger prying into my personal business as to the whys of my situation. Maybe he was an actor being directed by the Queen. I was very reluctant to share, after all I had just met the man. And I trusted no one. The tour ended and Mr. John stood on the steps of the front porch. He turned to me as he stepped down.

"Look, I know that your ex is going to auction this place off if it does not sell soon," he said, leaning his head to the right.

"How do you know anything about us?" I quickly snapped. I was so taken aback by his words.

"I have done my research. I know you are going through a really bad divorce. I know you have two boys and that you are a nurse and can't afford to maintain this house and acreage alone." He spoke without catching a breath. Then he told me that he would like to be my friend and help me. He reached for my arm, and I took a step back.

"I also know that you have a wife and two children," I admonished. "If you are interested in buying this house, you can contact my realtor. It is time for you to go now."

Without another word, he turned and walked to his car and left. I was totally disgusted to the point of being sick at my stomach. What was this guy up to? Who had told him about my house? My focus was my two children and to escape the clinches of the Black's saga alive.

A few days passed, and my phone rang. It was the realtor on the other end.

"Good news, Sandra. Mr. John has made an offer on the house."

Surprisingly, it was for the amount that we had listed.

Thirty-Two

I could hardly believe that the house, which had been the dream house I had wanted all my life, finally sold. I was fine with that because there were absolutely no good memories made in that house. I only had memories of torture, hate, fear and evil things that were said and done to me there. I had no peace in that house, ever. The house was never the home that I had dreamed of having. I was ready to close the curtain on that chapter of my life. As I did one last final walk through, I realized that God was preparing the beginning of my escape.

It was almost April. I only had to the end of April to sell the house of my dreams or it would be auctioned off. Mama had helped me find a little three-bedroom house that a friend's daughter at her work had for sell. It was in a neighborhood close to the school that the boys would attend. A tiny house with a large overgrown backyard and a big wooden porch that extended the length of the house. Now it belonged to me. I had never lived in a neighborhood. I was used to the big open fields and the large extending sky overhead. The farm I grew up on had seventy-two acres of land and no close neighbors. My dream house sat secluded in the middle of twenty-eight acres with no close neighbors. I was not at all excited about living between two other houses and directly across the street were neighbors as well. I was very private and wanted to stay that way.

Mama and I stood in the small house awaiting the furniture from the dream house to arrive. I ached. Overwhelmed with feelings of hopelessness, apprehension, panic and terror all wrapped in hate as I walked through the tiny house. I referred to it as a cracker box compared to my big dream house. It was several miles from my home place, away from Mama and Daddy, my rescue team and safety net. I collapsed into Mama's arms as we waited together and sudden flashes of the horrible things Charles had done to me came across my mind. I began to quiver. There was no way I could share with Mama the gruesome details of the role I had played in the saga of the Queen's drama. I tried to pull myself together as the movers pulled in the drive. The boys had remained safe with Grandmama until I could get the furniture arranged and a few things put away. Mama and I worked for hours arranging things in the new house. Mama encouraged me to think of it as a new beginning, a fresh start. Mama was not aware of the haunting promise Charles had made to me.

"If I can't have you, no one will."

It suspended over me constantly, like a thick fog. That impending danger was always present. There was clearly not any feeling of peace, excitement or a fresh start. Would I ever be free? He was still in my head, and he knew it. I knew that God was working on my complete escape plan, but realized it was still a work in progress. Oh, God, please keep me and my babies safe, I prayed.

A couple of hours later, Daddy arrived with the boys. They hopped out of Pawpaw's truck and ran straight to me. I tried very hard to act like that was where I wanted to be, so the boys would not pick up on my deep sadness. No way did this feel like where we belonged. I felt I'd had everything stolen from me and I was so afraid that the Queen would not stop until she had taken the only thing that mattered to me...my two boys. As the night drew near, my anxiety level increased. Mama and Daddy would soon have to go and leave me and the boys on our own. I had such a feeling of uneasy desperation. Afraid of the unknown, I put the boys in my bed with me and locked all the doors to the outside and on the inside. I sat up in the middle of the bed all night with the boys snuggled as close as I could get them and I watched them sleep. All alone in a strange place, it felt so far from the security of Daddy and Mama. I listened to the silence. Distant unfamiliar sounds of animals barking, cars passing, crickets chirping in unison seemed to be amplified. Finally, a hint of daylight appeared from a tiny opening behind the tightly drawn curtain. I blinked my eyes to readjust from the darkness. I sat beyond exhausted, staring at the two most beautiful children I had ever seen. Tears of guilt and remorse streamed down my face as I looked at two little innocent faces that certainly did not deserve to live like this. I vowed I would love and protect them no matter what it took.

I quietly slipped to the kitchen to prepare their breakfast. I had taken vacation time from work for the move. I would drive the boys, Alex, age seven, and Noah, age five, to their private school across to the west side of town. They attended prekindergarten and kindergarten there. I would return to pick them up in the afternoon. This would be their last year at the private school, because Charles refused to pay his half of the tuition. I spoke with the teachers and the school authority to ensure that no one could pick the boys up but me. The fear was always there that the Queen would somehow retrieve the boys and I would not be able to find them.

It was quiet an adjustment for me to move from my dream house to a tiny cracker box but I was determined to survive. I had returned to work and was trying hard to adjust to the tiny new house and being away from my security zone. There was never a peaceful time for me. I was not ignorant to the fact that the Queen would not bow out and close the curtain on her long-drawn-out saga. That was just not her style at all.

Thirty-Three

"Sandra, we are taking Grandmama to the emergency room," Mama's voice was fragile. "She had an event where she passed out and was unresponsive for a brief period of time."

"I will meet you there," I said.

I quickly gathered the boys up and headed to the hospital to meet Daddy and Mama who were driving Grandmama there. She was admitted to the hospital and was to have surgery once she was stable enough. I was beside myself with worry. I had always leaned on Grandmama for support. She was my confidant. I could not imagine my life without her, especially with all I was going through.

A week had passed, and I had worked my shifts in the NICU. I took turns with Mama and Daddy staying at the hospital. Grandmama's condition seemed to have worsened, so she was moved to the ICU. I went often to the break area to drink coffee to help me stay awake through the night.

"Hello," he said in a soft voice.

I turned to see who was speaking and it was a security guard that also worked at the hospital.

"Do you mind if I join you for a cup of coffee?"

He sat down, not waiting for me to answer.

"I've seen you around a lot lately," he said, stirring his coffee.

"One of the most important people in my life is in the ICU," I said.

"I understand, my grandmother passed not long ago, and I was devastated. We were very close, like you and your Grandmama."

It never dawned on me to ask how he knew I was very close to Grandmama, or how he knew she was the important person in the ICU.

"It was nice talking to you," I said with a taut smile. "I need to get back to the waiting area in case Grandmama needs me."

Several days continued with Grandmama in the ICU. Noticeably, that same security guard was at every turn I made. He stood five feet nine inches tall, with kind of long dark hair, and of course, the uniform was nice. This was a most vulnerable time for me as I felt that my entire world was in a violent whirlwind. Would it ever be good again? I had lost so much in the past three years. I felt like maybe God had sent this young man to be my friend, since I might lose my Grandmama like he had lost his. I felt that God was sending him into my life because he had to take Grandmama.

On February 17, 1984, I was with Grandmama as she took her last breath. I felt an unrelenting harsh pain like never before. I loved Grandmama and now she was not going to be by my side. The one person on this earth that really understood me, and she had to leave me. Daddy was already on his way to relieve me, when I phoned to tell him that Grandmama was getting worse. As Daddy entered the ICU, he could not contain his hurt. The anguish on his face, as tears welled up in his eyes, was more than I could bear. This was the first time that I had ever seen Daddy cry from so much pain. We held each other as we said our goodbyes to someone that was so cherished by both of us. Daddy was her baby boy and he had always taken good care of his mom. He loved her deeply. All the family loved her as she was so special to all of us. The family would never be the same. The loss of Grandmama and seeing Daddy so devastated was almost more than I could take. All I could think about was getting to my boys and holding them as tight as I could. Please, Lord, do not let anyone take them from me, I prayed quietly as the uncontrollable tears flowed. I hoped that someday my boys would grow up to love me and take care of me like Daddy had loved and cared for Grandmama. As Daddy and I walked down the long dark hall just before daybreak, I noticed the security guard approaching. He just walked quietly by us.

I had taken a few days off from work for the funeral and to be with my family. I would not let the boys out of my sight. As my family and friends gathered to say their last goodbyes at the visitation, I turned and there stood the Queen. I froze. What was she doing here? I immediately scanned the room for my boys and found them safe with my brother. The Queen walked up to me with that notorious smile across her face.

"I'm here to get the boys," she smirked. "They do not need to be here. They are too young."

I could hardly contain myself. How dare she come here at a time like this and act as though she was concerned.

"No," I said. "I want my boys to stay with me. They belong with me. They loved Grandmama and they need closure."

She turned and exited stage left. That was the first time I had ever confronted her with a "no," face to face. I shivered all over as though I had just taken an ice plunge in the depth of winter. I had known that it was just a matter of time before the Queen re-entered the stage for the continuation of her play. It had only been two months since the divorce papers were served. I was surprised that she had held off that long.

Thirty-Four

I had so much on my mind and had been beaten down so badly by Charles that my self-esteem was at a point where I did not entertain the thought of any kind of relationship with anyone. Oddly enough, it seemed that the security guard was in hot pursuit of me. He was at every corner I turned. It was obvious that he was intentional with his locations. I remained polite and always willing to engage in small talk with him, as I did with a lot of people I saw around the hospital daily. I certainly was not interested in a relationship with him or any other man. My world was upside down and my only focus was my children.

I had only been in the tiny new house less than a month when it began. I had not been comfortable since day one. I felt as if someone was watching me all the time. I continued to let the boys sleep in my bed. I would stay awake until the state of exhaustion overtook me. Then it began. A rattling noise outside my bedroom window was like the sound of a destructive warning. I was so frightened. I did not have a gun to protect me and my children. They would have to get through me to get to my children, I thought to myself as I sat holding a wooden bat. This went on night after night.

I came out early one morning to take my boys to school on my way to work. It was one of those moonless nights and still very dark. Walking toward my car, I stepped on something very soft in a bag on the ground. I quickly stepped backward and opened the car door to get some light. It was my cat. Someone had killed my cat and placed it in a bag by my car door. I immediately became upset, but I did not want my boys to see the cat. I made sure they were buckled in their seats, got in, and drove away. After I dropped my boys at school, I phoned Daddy and told him what happened. He knew I was unnerved by the quiver in my voice.

"Who would do such a thing?" I cried. "Daddy, will you please teach me to shoot a gun? I need to feel like I can protect us."

"Do you have a gun?"

"No, but come payday, I am going to get one."

"Of course, I'll teach you, but you must promise to keep it locked safely away from the boys."

Daddy reassured me that we would get to the bottom of this. He removed the cat so the boys would not see it. Leaving me to somehow explain to them why the cat just up and left. I could hardly wait for my shift to end at the hospital. I was more than anxious to get to my boys and go home to check on Useless, our dog. He was a cute little, long-haired white dog that the boys and I loved. He was so adored by the boys. He was their playmate. I am clearly an animal person. I loved and took good care of my animals. I treated them as though they were family. I tried to act normal in front of the boys so they would not be afraid. By bedtime I was already exhausted from the emotional day. I had called and called Useless, but he did not respond. That was not normal for Useless. He loved me and the boys as much as we loved him. Oh, please, Lord, do not let anyone hurt Useless.

I had the day off from work the next day, but I was totally withered from no sleep. I took the boys to school and came back home. I wanted to try to sleep a couple of hours. Soon as I drove back in, I could see Useless. He was trying to come across the back yard, but was weighted down and could hardly walk. I ran to him as fast as I could with tears streaming down my face. Someone had painted Useless with green and orange paint. I knew he would die if I didn't get the paint off. I quickly called Daddy. When he pulled up, I was holding Useless and sobbing. He drove us to the vet, and we were able to rescue Useless from this horrible act. The paint was very toxic and Useless would not have survived much longer. Daddy paid the vet bill, but Useless had to remain there for a couple of days.

I broke down on our way home. I felt like I was at the end of my rope. I told Daddy about all the other things, the rattling at the bedroom window, the cat and now the dog. I felt like all of it was a warning. How far would Charles and the Queen push me? Daddy told me to phone the police every night if I had to and to have them document that they came and what was going on. There needed to be a record of the things that were happening.

I hated living so far away from Mama and Daddy, but I remembered that Charles had told me I could not hide anywhere. He would always find me no matter what! I was thrown out of my thoughts at the shrill ringing of the phone.

"Good morning, Baby Girl, you ready to do some target practicing."

"The sooner the better."

"Well, come on down to the farm and I will teach you."

I was anxious to get this training done, hoping I would feel better if at least I could try to protect my boys from harm. Daddy was so proud of me, because I was actually a very good shooter. Charles would never have imagined that I would even attempt shooting a gun. The Queen had convinced him I was just a weakling.

I never slept a sound sleep. I only gave in to complete devastation and exhaustion.

A few nights later, it began again, the rattling under my bedroom window. It frightened me so badly, I sat straight up in bed and dialed 911.

"Please send someone quickly," I whispered with a terrified voice. "They are at my bedroom window in the back of my house. Hurry, please."

"Yes, ma'am, help is on the way," the operator assured me.

The doorbell rang and the officer announced it was the police. I opened the door in complete devastation. I shared with them all I had been enduring. I told them about the rattling under my window, my cat and the dog and not being able to sleep.

"We have looked all around your house and found nothing suspicious. We will do extra patrol of the area through the nights for a while. Do not hesitate to call 911," the officer instructed.

"Thank you for coming. Please don't forget to patrol frequently."

He made a report stating they did not find anything unusual. A few days later, I came out the front door and lying to the side of the steps was a hand full of grapes. What in the world? I wondered as I looked around. I walked around the house and found grapes at every door and window all the way around. I immediately called 911 as the officer had instructed me to do. This was like a warning to me that someone was watching me.

"There is nothing we can do, unless we actually catch someone in the act of placing the grapes there," the officer stated. Two different officers than before had answered the call.

"Will you please make a report for documentation?" I requested.

"Of course," one of them said.

"Thank you."

"Don't hesitate to call. I know that you are frightened. We will be close by."

I busily got to work hanging thick quilts that Grandmama had made over each window, where no one could see in. I even covered the French doors going out to the deck on the back of the house. It looked like a dark dungeon, but I felt like it was what I had to do. I became overly protective of the boys.

Charles insisted on visitation with them even though he refused to pay his child support. I had even taken another job on my off days from the hospital to make ends meet. I was working the weekend's sixteen hours shifts, so I did not have to be away from my boys as much. When they played their softball games on the weekends, I saved my lunch breaks and rushed to the ball field just to see Alex and Noah at their turn to hit the ball. Then I rushed back to work. I loved them so much and I loved seeing them enjoy playing ball. I wanted to be there to cheer them on. Their coach volunteered to transport Alex and Noah to their practices and their games. I was so grateful for him.

Things had been quiet for a couple of weeks. Useless was back home and his playful self again. He brought such joy to our family. But the overwhelming hovering of evil became real from time to time. I kept the windows covered. Once, when the boys were watching a movie, I was on my way down the hall to the laundry room with a load of clothes. I stopped dead in my tracks and backed up to the room where the boys were. I immediately dialed 911.

"This is Sandra Phoenix at—"

The operator interrupted me. "Help is on the way."

"Please hurry, he is coming in my back door."

The police arrived in time to catch the man at the back door. He had just been released from prison that week. As the police questioned him, it was obvious he had been drinking. His parents lived across the street from us, but I had never met them or him. The police looked around and they noticed an imprint in the tall grass in the back yard, like someone had been lying down. They felt like this guy had been laying there watching me. They arrested him and took him to jail that night, because he was on parole having just been released from prison earlier in the week.

About four hours later that night I received a phone call from a friend at the police station.

"Just called to tell you to be careful because the guy they arrested was released. He had been in prison for rape."

"Thanks for telling me."

I was in a state of shock. Hearing that news brought back that horribly terrifying night when I was raped by Charles. I did not close my eyes at all that night.

The next day I was off from work and an investigator from the police department dropped by to speak with me. He just so happened to be the husband of a friend from the hospital. He was there to share more information about my neighbor across the street. "Sandra, I advise you to stay inside as much as possible. Do not cut your grass in shorts, and be aware of your surroundings when you are coming in and going out. I know this may be upsetting for you, but I feel like it is just a matter of time before this man rapes again."

Turns out, the criminal across the street had gotten off on a loophole in his case.

"We are watching him very closely. Here is my number if you need anything, call." That officer had not a clue just how upsetting it was for me. I felt as though I was once again a prisoner at a war camp just waiting for the evil enemy to attack me. I could not stand the thought of a man like that touching me or coming near my boys. Did Charles have anything to do with this man scaring me? I just didn't understand. How much more? Would I ever have peace again?

A few days rocked on and it began again, the rattling under the window. I did not hesitate to call 911. Once again, the officers found nothing. I thought maybe if I called the police enough someone would eventually help me.

I told Daddy about what had happened over the past few days.

"Get the boys in the bedroom and lock the doors. Do not come out tonight."

He had a plan. He was not a man to break the law for no reason, but he was old school. Men just did not hurt women, especially their wives. Daddy was certain that Charles and the Queen were working to break me completely down. I could not physically keep going with no sleep, and the anxiety was overwhelming me. I was tough. I had grown up with three brothers, but there was only so much I could handle. Daddy parked his car at a church way down the road from my house. When it got dark, he came with his gun and hid under my deck on the back side of the house near the bedroom window. It was not long at all when the three young boys came with their empty paint cans to make the rattling noise. They laughed as they shook the cans. One of the young boys had a gun. How surprised they were when they turned to face a gun pointed in their faces. I heard all the commotion and went out to check on Daddy.

He yelled, "Call 911."

When the police arrived, they refused to take the boys to jail because they were juveniles. Even though one of them had a loaded gun, they still refused to take him in. The boys told the policemen that my ex-husband had paid them to scare and harass me. I told the officers that they had no idea what my children and I had been through and I wanted to press charges. They still refused to take them to jail. Daddy felt they had put the fear of God in the boys. After the police drove away, Daddy explained to them that if there was a next time, he would see to it that they would not get away with what they had done. He assured them that he would be the judge and jury and it would not end well for them. So, it would behoove them to stay away from me and my ex-husband. I knew that it had to have been the next act in the Queen's play and Charles had a huge part in it. What would they do next? He had always known that I was afraid of the dark, even since I was a little girl. He always seemed to attack me where he knew it would hurt the most. The Queen and her leading man were trying to wear me to a breaking point and make my life as miserable as possible. They thought tactics like that would set it up for them to parade in and sweep my boys away. I was certain that was their plan all along.

Things seemed to have quieted down for a few weeks. I was coming in from the store while the boys were at school. I was unloading my groceries, when suddenly the man from across the street jumped around my car and grabbed my arm.

"I just want to talk to you," he said. "I won't hurt you." He seemed frustrated and angry. I gasped for breath, jerked away from his grip on my arm. Dropping my groceries, I ran into the house and locked the door. Frantically, I called 911 and the investigator. They responded very quickly. I shared with the investigator the things I had gone through and asked if they thought Charles was encouraging this guy to scare me. They felt that my neighbor would be going back to jail very soon, and I would not have to be afraid much longer.

The next morning, the investigator called to inform me that the neighbor was locked up again and would be for a long time. He did not share with me what the man had done. I really didn't want to know. I just thanked God that he did not hurt me or my boys. On my way to pick up the boys from school, I stopped in a neighborhood store. The clerk and another man were talking about my neighbor being arrested for rape last night. I put down my items and rushed out to my car. I trembled and shivered as I thanked God that he did not hurt me. Then I said a prayer for his victim. I knew I had to get out of that neighborhood. But how?

Financially, I could not make a move. Charles refused to pay his child support, and I was struggling. I would have to make it the best I could for now. I talked to my attorney about the child support not being paid and all the things I had dealt with and endured. I shared my concerns about the boy's visitation with the Queen without their dad. This was the third attorney that I had hired to help me. I seemed to get no help legally because of the inside pull of his aunt at the courthouse. Every attorney I hired seemed to work for Charles at my expense. My current attorney required a hefty retainer and decided to take him back to court for increase and back child support. I was always leery at messing with Charles about any issue, but I did feel the children deserved to be taken care of and Charles had drastically changed their lifestyle. The court papers were filed.

The doorbell rang. It was Ms. Ruth from my attorney's office. I was surprised. No one from his office had ever been to my home. As I welcomed her in, Ms. Ruth could see the puzzled look on my face. Her warm smile reassured me.

"Everything is okay," she said. "I needed to do a walkthrough of your home because Charles has filed a countersuit. He claims that the children are not being taken care of and that the neighbors will testify that you dance naked in front of your windows at night."

I stood motionless. I could not believe what I was hearing. My house was always immaculate and there was food in the fridge. Ms. Ruth explained to me that this was routine procedure when a claim like that was made. I still had the quilts over all the windows and doors. I explained why.

"I do not know any of my neighbors. How could they be so cruel?"

"Money talks, Honey."

A few days later, there was another knock on the door. I slowly and carefully cracked the door open. An older lady stood there.

"May I speak with you a moment?" she asked. "I am your neighbor from across the street."

I stepped onto the porch, closing the door behind me. The lady told me how sorry she was that her son had bothered me. She looked around and leaned in closer.

"I thought you would want to know that a private investigator named Henry came to our home asking questions about you, your visitors, your children, and when you come and go. He had visited all the neighbors on the street.

"He is working for my ex-husband," I sighed.

"I told him that from what I could see you were a hard-working mom that took very good care of your children." She nodded for emphasis. "I will testify for you in court if you need me to. Again, I am so sorry for what my son did to you."

"Thank you," I said as I touched her hand. "I will be calling on you for help."

I continued to work, and became more aware of my surroundings. I was very observant of the small red vehicle that seemed to follow me everywhere. Henry did not even try to be secretive about his assignment.

I had just got off from my second job and picked up the boys. We headed home and discussed our plans for "pizza and a movie" night. As I entered my home, I saw that my furniture had been rearranged. I quickly gathered the boys to the movie room and dialed 911. Would this saga of never-ending torture ever cease? Why couldn't Charles just man up and do what was right for his children and leave us alone?

Thirty-Five

Meantime, whenever I was at work, J. T. Dakota, the security guard, was always around. I was so tired and distraught most of the time, I did not even realize what was happening. He was heavily manipulating his way into my life. He knew all the things to say and the limits not to push. He would play his role very carefully. He was so sly with his methods of getting me to talk about what I was going through. I remained very private and well-guarded about my life and my children. J. T. had shared with me that he knew a lot of officers and had a lot of friends that could help protect me and my boys. He also worked as an emergency medic at the hospital. He seemed to make it his mission to get into my life quickly. But my focus was on my boys and keeping them safe. I was unhappy oftentimes when at work, because I wanted to be with my boys. That hovering cloud of impending doom seemed to always be in the near distance, just waiting for the right time.

While my attorney was preparing for court, Charles' attorney had met with him and insisted that I go to Atlanta with my boys and have a psychiatric evaluation. My attorney agreed at this point only if Charles would agree to do the same. The attorney's office setup an appointment for me and my boys for the following week.

Mama went with me and the boys to Atlanta for the psych evaluation. It was an all-day ordeal. However, the results of the report stated that the boys did not need to be left alone with the Queen and that even Charles needed a supervised visitation program to be able to see the boys. The evaluation was very costly for me, but I felt I had no choice. Once again, Mama and Daddy helped me financially. Charles refused to go for his evaluation. The ruse was just to put a hardship on me. I was glad in the end that I had gone, because the information gained ironically turned out to be beneficial for me and the boys.

My attorney had set up several depositions. Charles' was the last one needed. He postponed it several times. He finally completed his deposition, and my attorney phoned me immediately after.

"I insist that you take your boys and leave town until the day of the hearing," he said. "I understand that it is four days away, but I insist that you leave right away and tell no one where you are going."

There was such an urgency in his voice that fear spilled all through me. Doing what he recommended was very difficult for me, because I was scheduled to work and I had no extra money to travel. Where would I go? How would we eat and where would we stay? I immediately phoned my supervisor and explained I had an urgent crisis and needed time off. My supervisor was not at all understanding and was reluctant to give me time off.

"Well, I will just have to resign if you won't help me," I said. "I am begging. I do not want to lose my job, but the safety of my children is more important."

My supervisor reluctantly agreed to let me take the time off, but insisted I would have to make it up. I then phoned my cousin and explained to her what was going on. I had gone outside to make the calls, because I wondered if the Queen had bugged my house while rearranging the furniture. My cousin was deeply concerned.

"You can stay here at my house," she said. "I will take care of you and the boys. Don't even bother packing. I will buy clothes for all of you when you get here."

I grabbed my purse, my keys and strapped the boys in the car and left immediately. On my way out, my phone rang. It was J. T.

"Hey, what's going on?" He asked.

"Oh, nothing just taking a day or two off. I'll return in a few days."

I was so terrified my voice was trembling. Thank God I was very vague about where I was going. It never entered my mind how he knew something was going on. Me and my boys remained safe at my cousins for four days, but in my mind, I could hear Charles telling me that no matter where I hid, he would find me. I still sat in the middle of the bed with the boys as close to me as I could get them and never closed my eyes. It was a very long four days, and I was emotionally worn out. The boys and I returned the morning of the hearing date. Daddy met me in town to get the boys and I continued to my attorney's office. As I sat there in the waiting area, the door opened and Charles' attorney came out. He turned and shook my attorneys' hand and they both were laughing as they looked my way.

"You can come in now, Ms. Black," my attorney stated.

"Your hearing date has been postponed again."

I just wanted to scream as loud as I could. What had just happened? Had his attorney just bought my attorney off? I was livid.

"You had me leave town and I almost lost my job. For nothing? If he was such a threat to us then, what is different now?" I expressed eagerly with tears.

"Charles had voiced disturbing statements of concern in his deposition, and we felt he might carry them out. That is why I had you leave. You will need to be extra cautious and observant, and we will have extra police outside your home as we try to reschedule the hearing quickly."

I left my attorney's office horrified. What had Charles said? Was he going to hurt me and take my boys? When Charles said something like that through frustration and anger that ran all the way through him, I did not doubt that he meant what he said. I was convinced at that time in my life that he had the connections and the means to carry out his threats.

When I arrived home, I found that all the lights in my house had been turned on. I knew that even in my haste to leave that I had not left a single light on, especially not every light in the house. It was just a message to let me know that they had been inside my home again. I could see the Queen sauntering around her abode like she had just been crowned. I quickly phoned Daddy and asked if me and the boys could stay there for a few days. Of course, the answer was yes. At least I felt safe there, and I knew Daddy would not let anything happened to us.

The hearing day finally arrived. I always dreaded the thoughts of having to see Charles face to face with his inappropriate smile smirked across his face. As my attorney and I entered the courtroom, I took a panoramic view and there was no Charles in the room. My heart sank, even though I did not want to see him, I wanted this hearing to end. As the judge entered the courtroom, Charles' attorney stated that Charles would not be there, and he would represent him. The judge was new, and he found him in contempt of court and ordered the back child support to be paid. He did not address any of the other issues except visitation would continue as it is. I knew that this meant nothing except now I had another huge attorney's bill to pay. Nothing had changed. Charles and the Queen would continue to antagonize me as they scripted the next act of their play.

Thirty-Six

It had been a busy chaotic shift at the hospital. I stepped outside on my break to get some fresh air. I was constantly weighted down with the dominating thought of the safety of my boys. I continually prayed that God would somehow end this insufferable season of my life. Oddly enough, as I turned to go back into the hospital, there stood the security guard. It was as though he knew my every move. This should have sent up a red flag, but at that point I was still so naïve I never entertained the thought of any deception within him. I really did not even know him that well.

"I see a troubled look that you harbor in your eyes," he said. "Look, you can trust me with whatever it is. I have a lot of connections that could help you. Just let me help you."

I shared with J. T. about all the lights being on in my house when I came home from hiding out before the hearing. He offered to stay at my house while me and the boys stayed at Daddy and Mama's, to see if he could catch someone. I thought that was so sweet of him. What could it hurt? If I had only known!

It was a beautiful moonlit night. I made my way back to the hospital to work the night shift, because someone had called out sick. I had worked my twelve-hour day shift and gone home to sleep for a few hours, so I could return for the night shift. As I turned left to go to the employee parking lot, something jolted my car with a loud crunch. I was stunned. I had no idea what the noise and the jar to my car was from. I learned later that a motorcycle with two people riding it came speeding out of nowhere and crashed into the right rear panel of my car. I stopped and looked in the rear-view mirror. I saw a guy lying in the street to the side of the rear of my car. I immediately jumped out of my car and ran to kneel by his side. He was holding his leg up in the air and shouting that he was going to sue me for this. His foot dangled to the side of his leg. The EMTs were on the scene immediately since the accident happened right in front of the emergency room. As they wheeled the stretcher carrying the young man by me, he had them stop.

"I will sue you," he said angrily. "You will pay for this."

I could not find any words to reply. I just stood there in the midst of all the flashing red and blue lights. A blurry chaos spun all around me. I was in a state of shock. I stood all alone, trying to comprehend what had just happened. A policeman came over to me and told me to move my car over to the parking lot.

"I can't do that," I said with trembling lips.

"You must do it," he said. "If you do not immediately get back in and drive, you might not be able to overcome the fear you are experiencing right now. You may never be able to drive again."

I did as he asked. He retrieved my information to complete his report. As he was questioning me, a doctor friend walked up and gave me a hug.

"Everything is going to be okay," he said in a comforting voice. "Do you have someone you can call? Your dad, a brother or someone that could come help you?"

Daddy was at work, so I phoned my brother. He was enroute immediately. While I waited for him to arrive, I looked around and noticed J. T. mingling in the crowd. Then I noticed Charles riding by very slowly as if he wanted me to know he was responsible. As he circled around again, I caught another glimpse of him. This time he had a woman with him, another nurse. I just turned in disgust feeling so defenseless.

By the time my brother arrived, I was free to go and could escape the mess. It was as though I was in a slow-motion scene. I could see their mouths moving but could not hear what all the people around me were saying. It was as if I was floating and none of it was real. The children were no doubt with the Queen, because their dad was circling the hospital without them. I was bombarded with fear and anxiety. Where were my boys? What would happen to the two people on the bike? Would I be charged? I replayed the events as my brother drove. I had sat through the whole red light behind another car turning. I had seen two people who I knew pass by me as I sat there waiting for the light to change. I knew I had witnesses that could prove I not run the red light. That's what I was accused of—running the red light. I was charged with failing to yield the right of way. The motorcycle had a whole other lane to avoid colliding into my car, but he chose to hit me. My brother took me to Mama and Daddy's. I did not sleep a wink. I was sitting in the recliner when Daddy opened the door and came in from work at the fire station. He knelt beside my chair and gave me a hug.

"It will be okay, Baby Girl."

He could always make me feel safe and secure. I just could not understand why so many bad things happened to me. Through my tears, I asked Daddy to take me to see the young man that had been hurt. That's just how I was, concerned and so caring of others. I could not accept that I was the reason someone had gotten hurt. Daddy took me to the hospital to see the guy that was in the wreck. He was someone that I had known from high school. He was very well known for his alcohol and drug use. I did not realize at the time of the wreck this was the same guy I knew. As I entered his hospital room, I told him I was sorry he had gotten hurt, and I wanted to check on him. With an inappropriate grin he once again told me he was going to sue me for everything I had. I immediately left the room. My head was spinning, my knees weak and trembling so hard I leaned against the wall to brace myself. Daddy rushed to my side.

"I didn't think this was a good idea, Baby Girl," he said as he held me close to his side. "Let's go home."

Once we arrived home, Daddy insisted that I try to sleep a little. I was totally exhausted—physically, emotionally and mentally. Later that afternoon, the television was on and they were reporting on my accident. A picture and details of the nurse who ran a red light injuring two people, one of which was a want-to-be celebrity. I could not believe it. I was appalled. It was all lies. How could they be allowed to air that information? They were judge and jury, poisoning other people's opinion about the accident. I was not guilty, and I would fight to prove it. I called the reporter that covered the story and told him that he did not present the truth. He said since I was driving a car, and a motorcycle was involved, I was automatically guilty. I knew that I was not guilty and I would fight to prove my innocence. Mama and Daddy were right beside me with their support. Could I cope through this battle? It would certainly not be easy.

Several weeks later, I was working my shift at the hospital and the phone rang. The secretary announced the call was for me. I made my way to the nurses' station to take the call.

"This is Nurse Black. How may I help you?"

The voice on the other end announced to me that this was the police station calling and I needed to turn myself in or they would come to the hospital and arrest me for the accident. I could hardly catch my breath to respond. After a brief pause, I told the officer I would come there. Through tears and accelerated breathing, I called Daddy and told him about the situation. He instructed me to stay there at the hospital and he would come to take me to the police station. Daddy knew all the policemen and was friends with the chief. Daddy arrived at the hospital and my supervisor released me from my shift to go with him. He had phoned the chief of police before picking me up. Upon our arrival at the police station, the chief was waiting to greet us in the parking lot. He was very compassionate and considerate. He listened intently as I explained what had happened. He told Daddy he would escort me to the jail to be booked and he would stay with me throughout the entire process.

"Hud, you follow behind us in your truck."

As the chief escorted me out to his patrol car, he started to put me in the back seat of the car. He noticed how pale and weak I had become.

"Never mind," he said. "I don't think you are a hardened criminal. You can ride up front with me."

I said nothing and followed his lead. As I sat down in the front seat, I looked down at the paperwork, "State vs Criminal Sandra Phoenix Black." I became hysterical. I was at my breaking point. Was I going to wake up? I was a nurse. My role in life was to "Do No Harm." Could I hold it together enough to deal with what was ahead of me? The chief pulled the car over and motioned for Daddy to pull over.

"Hud, she needs you to ride with us," the chief explained. "I will bring you back to your truck later."

Daddy got in the back seat and assured me that it would be okay, and he would not leave me. The chief escorted me into the booking area. Daddy could not go any farther with me. He promised to get a bond for my release. The big automatic iron door rolled slowly and made a clanging sound with every inch of movement. It creeped to the other side of the opening and came to its resting place with an even louder clank, which announced my chilling final destination. I tearfully looked at Daddy on the other side as though I would never see him again. Suddenly, my boys' faces flashed across my mind. I knew the Queen would enjoy using my arrest as leverage to take my boys from me. The three guards behind the iron door were so mean to me. As they took my fingerprints, they went back and forth arguing about what they thought my bond amount should be set at.

"Oh, no. That is not high enough for what she has done," one of them was eager to share. Oh, I think it should be this or that. They all tossed around their ideas. They were still going back and forth as I was placed in a holding cell.

"Please, don't close the door and lock it," I begged. "Daddy is right out front fixing it where I can go home with him."

All of the guards looked at each other and laughed. This seemed to be their cheap thrill for the day. I will never forget how they treated me, as if they were some angelic beings flying so far above a terrified earthly creature. I was released after a couple of hours. The chief drove me and Daddy back to his truck as promised and I went home with my Daddy.

Daddy immediately went to work investigating the accident.

The next day at work, J. T. found me on my break. He shared with me that he knew an attorney that owed him a favor and he would help me. I told him that I could not afford an attorney. He assured me that he would go with me and that money would not be an issue. I hesitated.

"Okay," I relented.

A little while later he returned and had arranged a meeting with the attorney on my next off day. I had not heard of this attorney, but apparently, he was very well known in our small town.

A couple of days later, on my off day, I met J. T. at the new attorney's office. The attorney, Mr. Clint, agreed to help me. The plan included a jury trial where I would prove my innocence. I did not know until now that J.T. had witnessed the cousin of the injured guy telling him that he had told him to get the headlight on his motorcycle fix. So, Mr. Clint immediately had the headlight from the wrecked motorcycle sent off to the crime lab. He had multiple witnesses already lined up to testify. Two of the witnesses agreed to testify to the fact that the motorcycle had passed them at a high rate of speed just before colliding with my car. From the point of where the motorcycle had passed the witnesses, my attorney was able to figure the rate of speed they were traveling upon impact with my car. The speed well exceeded the speed limit in that area. Furthermore, I could not possibly have seen the motorcycle, because I had already made my turn before he was even visible.

Three weeks later while I was waiting for trial, there was a knock on my door. I opened it to find an officer standing there to serve me with papers. I was being sued by the want-a-be-celebrity for ruining her career as a model. She claimed that the bruise on her leg interfered with her modeling career. The papers also stated that I had killed a man with my car in years past. I could not get to the phone fast enough. I nervously called my attorney and Daddy and J. T.

"Mr. Clint, please," I said. "This is Sandra Black, and I need to speak with Mr. Clint."

"Hello."

"Mr. Clint, this is Sandra Black," I said quickly. "I just got served with papers suing me and saying I killed someone."

"Just calm down, Sandra. Bring me the papers as soon as you can. I will wait for you at my office."

"Okay," I sighed. "I will be there soon as I can."

My voice echoed how distraught I felt. I could envision being locked up for something I did not do. I would lose my boys! My boys were always at the forefront of my mind in every situation. I phoned Mama to get my boys, and I rushed to the attorney's office. As he read the papers, he asked me if I was sure the prior incident was not referring to me. He also asked if I had ever had amnesia. I was beyond frustrated. I paced back and forth. The attorney's secretary was trying to contact the law office that had issued the papers that had been served to me.

When I had arrived at my attorney's office earlier a man came in right behind me. I had not paid much attention to him at first. The secretary asked if she could help him.

He said, "No. I'm with her," referring to me.

I recognized him as the man that had been following me and had interviewed all my neighbors. What was he doing here? He never spoke to me, he just sat and listened. For three hours, I stood my ground—I had not killed anyone. The mystery man sat and waited. Finally, the attorney that had issued the papers phoned back and was put on speaker phone. He stated that it was a typographical error that had been made. Those papers were actually supposed to be served to someone else. They had been mixed in with the want-a-be-celebrity's claim by mistake. Mr. Clint explained to him that we would be countersuing the girl and his law firm for the mental anguish and torment I had endured because of the error. The other attorney said that would not be necessary that he would take care of it. They would not follow through with their suit at all. I was so relieved and exhausted after hours of agonizing stress over being doubted. My attorney explained that he had to ask those questions. I thanked him for helping me. He hugged me and told me to go get my boys and get some rest. I, and my follower (Henry), left Mr. Clint's office at the same time, with not a word spoken between us. He exited stage left with a smile and a tilt of his head.

I went straight to Mama and Daddy's to get my boys. At times like these they were the only thing that kept me sane. They were my reason for living without them I could not have survived any of the things that had been dealt me. I had made a promise to always be there to keep them safe no matter what, and I had every intention of keeping my promise.

Throughout all the drama and chaos, J. T. had been calling me and coming around a lot. It was certainly not at my request. He just seemed to be everywhere I turned. I did feel more secure with him around. He always said he and his friends could help me keep the boys safe. I fell hook-line-and-sinker for that one. I had been through so much I needed a little reprieve from it all. I was not at all interested in a relationship with a man. Especially not a romantic relationship after all the abuse suffered at the hands of a deranged man that was supposed to love me. I could never remember Charles telling me he loved me, not even once. I could never remember us even laughing together. Regardless, I was willing to do what it took for my boys to be safe, even if it meant pretending to like someone.

The trial lasted three long days. J. T. was eventually called to testify on my behalf. He stated what he knew about the motorcycle and the guy that was injured. The investigation had revealed that injured guy made a living by having wrecks, suing the people involved, and collecting the insurance money. The want-a-be-celebrity was actually a stripper who worked the Atlanta hot spots. They had both been drinking the night of the accident. The crime lab proved the head light on the motorcycle was not working prior to the accident. The speed at which they were traveling was well above the speed limit in that area. The jury did not deliberate very long at all, less than an hour. The judge called for the jurors to return.

"Have you reached a verdict?"

"Yes, Your Honor."

My heart was beating out of my chest as my attorney and I stood. The foreman read the verdict out loud.

"Your Honor, we, the Jury, unanimously find the Defendant not guilty."

"You are free to go, Mrs. Black," the judge declared and slammed his gavel. "This Court is adjourned."

Daddy, Mama and I were all elated. I just wanted to run and hide with my boys, so no one else could hurt me anymore.

The next day I met with my attorney to thank him.

"I don't know how I will ever be able to repay you," I said.

"There was never any charge," he replied. "Go, take care of yourself and your boys." He gave me a hug and wished us well.

Thirty-Seven

Up until this point, I had relied upon the comfort of having J. T. around for protection. He seemed to think he had become part of the family. That was his goal from the beginning. Now, he had a view from the inside out. There was so much about him that I still did not know. I would not learn his true identity until many years later.

I sat looking out the only window in the NICU where I worked. I saw J. T. engaged in a heated conversation with another security guard in the emergency parking lot. I wondered what it was about. An older nurse that had worked at the hospital for a very long time walked up next to me.

"Sandra, what are you watching so intently?"

She followed my gaze and peered out the window. "You know that is his wife, right?"

I was so shaken by that revelation I had to leave the room for a minute. I could not let anyone see that I was emotionally torn. What if the Queen found out that a married man was helping me? This was not like me to get myself involved with a married man. How could he have spent so much time with me? Following me around, calling, being at every corner I turned? How could his wife, who worked at the same hospital, not know?

The woman appeared masculine. She was heavy set with short blonde hair. Was my friend sure about this? This woman certainly did not look like a match for him. It was not very long at all until J. T. was standing at the door of the NICU. He motioned for me to come over to him. I stepped outside the door.

"Well," I raised my eyebrows. "Is everything okay with your wife? Things looked a little heated in the parking lot."

He acted surprised and said he could explain. I told him I never wanted to see him again. He still insisted he could explain.

"We are getting a divorce," he said quickly.

I just turned and walked away. He was very persistent in working his way into my life. He was not one to let up on following me and calling me. He constantly left message after message on my voicemail, notes on my car and at my home. At times, he was a plain out nuisance. Then something would happen again, and it was like he had a premonition that I would need him. He was always there at the right time. I noticed that he had even followed me out of town as though to protect me. He had really helped me with the attorney and the motorcycle case I had just gone through. When I confronted him about keeping silent about being a married man, he always seemed to have the answer I needed to hear. Pretending that he had begun to really care for me and my safety, as well as my boy's safety.

Thirty-Eight

Over the next few years, I was in and out of court with Charles and the Queen. He never paid his child support and the Queen was relentless in keeping her promise to destroy my life. If only I could have seen behind the curtain on the stage. I was just not able to contemplate the evil acts that the Queen and Charles could fabricate for the next dramatic entrance of their performance. I did not have that kind of blood running through my veins. Never could I have put together such an evil plot.

J. T.'s divorce was finalized a few months ago. This seemed to open the door for constant visitation from him, whether I agreed or not. I was so worn from the chaotic zigzagging maze of my life, there was no inner or outer peace for me. Within just a few months he began insisting that he and I begin looking for a larger home. He wanted to move in with us, so he could keep us safe. He knew that I had already set a goal to get away from our current neighborhood as soon as I could manage it. But I had not even considered expanding my world, which consisted only of me and my boys. It was obvious that Charles had diverted his full attention from me to a new lifestyle that included the other woman. At least, I thought that was true. The other woman was a nurse at the same hospital where I worked. It was a small-town hospital and rumors propelled from the top floor to the bottom and all in between at lightning speed. Co-workers did not mind sharing with me that they had seen Charles cruising around the hospital late at night waiting for his new woman to finish her shift. Little did they know that I had already witnessed their relationship the night of my wreck. It was not long before her identity was released to me from a co-worker who loved to gossip. I felt like she was awaiting my reaction to the information she shared, so she could spread even more rumors. I made it a point to act nonchalant in response to the news, as if I already knew the nurse's name was Mel. She stood solid at five feet eight inches, a very masculine stature. She even resembled the Queen. She drove a rugged looking open jeep. Nothing at all like I would picture the Queen approving of for Charles. She worked the adult intensive care on the same floor as I did. I was sure this was not a coincidence. The Queen did not seem to understand that I was elated to have Charles' attention off of me, even if for a little while. It would be a long time before I realized that was not the case. I had a very keen sense of intuition and often, I felt someone watching me. I was for sure right on track.

It had been two and a half years living in the tiny cracker box, and I had given in to a relationship with J. T., the security guard. He introduced me to a realtor that he was personal friends with that knew of a larger house that was in foreclosure and within my budget. The only drawback: it was on the west side of town. It was much farther away from Mama and Daddy, my support system, but I was desperate to get away from that neighborhood where so much had happened and I felt under constant surveillance.

Alex was nine years old and Noah was eight, when I moved them to the west side of town. They loved the house. It had more privacy and was at the end of a cul-de-sac. It had a fenced back yard for Useless. The boys had to deal with so much in their young lives that I really stressed about moving them to another school. The adjustment was certainly not an easy one, but I tried my best to make it easier for them.

The boys and I, and the security guard, lived in the new large house on the west side of town for less than a year. One afternoon, just as I began a late lunch, there was a knock on the door. I opened the door to greet another sheriff's deputy.

"Evening, Ma'am. I am looking for Sandra Phoenix Black."

"Yes, Sir, that's me,"

"I am serving you papers, Ma'am. Please sign here."

I quickly opened the papers and read. Not just Charles, but the Queen and Charles together, were suing me for custody of both my boys. The papers claimed that I was an unfit mother because I was allowing J. T. to live in the same house. There was no mention of the fact that J. T. lived in the large three-room basement. I was bewildered. I could envision the Queen twirling about in her domain chanting that she would soon have destroyed my world completely. This would be the Queen's most extreme performance yet. I shook so hard to the point of regurgitation. I could not imagine my life without my children. I felt as if my heart was stuck in my throat. I could hardly breathe. It was a few minutes before I could speak without the tremor in my voice. I had to gain enough composure to phone my attorney. Not expecting to speak directly to him when I phoned, I was relieved when he answered. He set an appointment for the next day to meet with me. Did he have information I was being served? Did he know I would be calling? I knew all along in the back of my mind it was just a matter of time. Therefore, I never let my guard down to the lurking evil and the impending danger that surrounded me no matter where I went or what I was doing. I constantly felt someone watching me. Even after all these years. Would I ever be free? How could anyone help me now? My boys were my reason for living, and no man was worth the risk of losing them. I met with my attorney the next morning. He began working on the case, but he did require me to bring a $2,000 retainer for him to help me. I did not have that kind of money, so he was willing to let me bring my whole paycheck to him on the upcoming Friday. I was more than devastated and beyond. I had bills. I knew I must ask Daddy for money. Of course, he would be more than willing. He and Mama would do anything for me and the boys. But I just hated having to ask. I felt at times that my attorney enjoyed asking me for money he knew I did not have. I often felt he was abusing me because he knew I was in a desperate situation and needed his help. After all, I was still paying on the bill for previous work he had done. I knew I had to ask J. T. to leave. Nothing was going to come before my two boys. I loved them bigger than life itself. In preparing the case my attorney followed up on leads about some illegal activity that Charles was involved in and that he had no home to take the boys to. He was living in a hangar where he housed his airplane. It seemed that Charles was always a step ahead of the sheriff's department when they were trying to locate him to serve him with a countersuit or to arrest him for contempt of court from a previous court hearing. He was extremely behind in paying his child support. I could not understand how he knew they were coming. "Every time he somehow knew." He had cleared his hangar completely out. His ex-girlfriend gave a statement that he was living there. There was nothing there when the deputies entered. I was confused to say the least. Even though J. T. had moved out, he was still coming around under the pretense of helping me. He asked for all the details of what the attorney had in mind and the strategies he planned to use against Charles. Of course, I told him. It took six months for the case to get close to starting. During this time my attorney contacted Mel for a deposition. Being years later, she had married a guy that J. T. new well, because he also worked at the same hospital. Mel and Roy were willing to meet with me. Mel said she was more than willing to testify for me against Charles. She had shared in her deposition that he was obsessed with my whereabouts and that he had plans to hurt me and do away with me. I had just thought that he had refocused his attention but all the while he always knew exactly where I was and what I was doing. That had never changed. But how did he know those things? How could he know everything I did? Charles really did not want the boys. He had said as much to me.

"You and the boys are holding me back from living the life I want," he stated.

He did not care enough to pay his child support. He never called the boys on their birthdays. So many times, he would say he was coming to get them, and they would sit waiting, but he never came. I could not remember a time when I saw him at their sports events. There was absolutely no doubt that this was a segment of the play that the Queen was delightfully directing. A promise she had made to me many years ago that she intended on keeping until the end. She loved the element of surprise when developing her strategy of attack on my life. I had to meet these people on their level. I was not going to surrender without a fight, that was for sure. Behind the scenes, I had a wonderful doctor friend that adored me and my boys. She had a baby boy and knew how torn I was about the thought of losing mine. My doctor friend developed a plan. She knew people and she had money. She proposed to help me escape with my boys. She arranged for a friend to meet me across the Mississippi Bridge. Her friend would take me, my boys and my brother underground. With her instructions, I made all the necessary arrangements for Daddy to have power of attorney for my house and belongings. I could not tell them where I was going, and I knew it would be a very long time before I would be able to see or communicate with them. My younger brother loved me enough to do the same. He was not going to let me and the boys go alone. I ached at the thought of what this would do to Mama and Daddy. We were all such a close loving family, but I had to take care of my boys. They were my life. Even through my worried, fearful, heartbroken eyes, my parents knew my heart. We said our goodbyes.

I loaded the car with a small number of belongings. My two boys; my brother, John; my very best friend, Ethel and I were loaded and ready to go. It was about a month prior to the court date of the custody hearing. We headed for Panama City Beach, Florida. I had devised a plan to go this route, because the boys and I went to Panama on vacation with my family in prior years. I hoped that Charles would not follow or have me followed there. I arranged for my best friend to ride back with a co-worker that was already vacationing there.

I cut our trip short, said goodbye to my best friend and headed on up the coast to New Orleans with my brother and my boys. I had never felt such anguish in my entire life. I did not want to die or leave my boys to evil people. Charles had promised that I could never hide well enough that he could not find me. That promise kept playing over and over in my head. He would kill me if he found me. I knew he would. The drive up the coast was terrible. Torrential rain beat against the windshield so badly the wipers could not keep up. Visibility was not conducive to safe travel. I was so tired. The boys were hungry, and we were lost in a really bad section of New Orleans. A section of town that everyone involved in planning the trip had warned me to avoid. I panicked. I had always been afraid of bridges, and we were stopped on one at the very top as it opened for a ship to pass underneath. I sat petrified waiting for the closure, so I could get off the bridge. I had only seen this type of bridge on TV, never in real life. Finally, we made it to the other side on land again. I pulled off the road and sat and cried. The boys were asking to go home, and I wanted to go home as much as they did. I needed to be close to my Mama and Daddy. I found a pay phone and called my doctor friend to ask her if I could just come back home.

"Of course, you can come home," she said. "But since it's late, go to my parents' house in New Orleans and spend the night. Things might look different in the morning."

"Okay, I am really tired."

My doctor friend phoned ahead, and her parents were waiting our arrival with a hot meal prepared and fresh towels for a relaxing hot shower. We ate, took our showers and I put the boys to bed. I sat and watched them sleep and prayed God would intervene and give me strength to fight the battle when I returned home. I knew that I needed God's help to win when I encountered Goliath and Satan.

The next morning, I was awake before anyone else. The parents of my doctor friend were such caring people and made me feel at ease there, but I knew I had to return home. I woke John and the boys. We said our thanks, and goodbyes and were on our way home. Even with the uncertainty of what waited ahead, I knew I had to go home. I drove a little way down the highway and at the first rest stop, I phoned Mama and Daddy to tell them we were on our way home. Of course, they were delighted and offered to do anything to help me win this battle. The rain had stopped and the day filled with sunshine. The boys were excited to be headed home.

I called my doctor friend once we arrived at home and explained my fear of being killed if Charles found out that I had taken the boys. The Queen would stage the scene and make Charles search until he found me. She was more than understanding. We were very close friends and I trusted her. She immediately devised another plan in the event that the court case did not go well. She would take the boys and get a head start and I would meet them later. She would have her underground contact waiting just in case we needed him. I never knew how much my friend had paid to help me, but I was more than grateful.

Thirty-Nine

The court battle for custody of my boys started. I knew deep down that out of all the things I had dealt with from the saga of the Queen's production, this would be the most difficult of all. This battle involved my whole world, my two boys. I had always put my boys first in my life, no matter the opinions of others who were quick to judge. I did what I did to ensure my boys were safe.

It would be a couple of years later, before I discovered the real truth of this act of the play directed by the Queen. I did not know it, but I was fighting a battle from the inside and the outside. I was determined. I was not the same meek little girl that Charles had captured years ago.

While preparing for the case, the boys had voiced that they did not want to go to their dad's house for visitation, especially little Noah. He cried and begged me not to make him go. They saw very little of their dad on visitation. It was always the Queen who picked them up and kept them.

J. T. still came around, even though he no longer lived here. He saw how upset the boys were about their visitation and began asking questions to uncover any abuse that might have happened there. I stood in the silence as the boys described what their visits were like with the Queen. I was capsized at what I heard. Inexplicable abuse aimed at little Noah more so than Alex. Broken bones, burns, puncture wounds and mental cruelty just to name a few things. I had always questioned why Noah came home hurt from his visitations and the story behind each incident certainly did not match up with what the boys now sharing. I was broken inside. The knowledge of the hurt and devastation my children endured was unbearable. I felt so guilty that all of this was aimed to destroy me through my children. I was determined to stop this saga. This was where the rubber meets the road for me. Hurting and torturing me was one thing, but to harm two innocent children was another. How could Charles leave the boys with the Queen? He knew what she had done to him. Why would he subject his own children to the same treatment? He was just as twisted as the Queen.

Little Noah had a favorite goat at the Black's house that he loved like a pet. The minute he got out of the car, he ran to find his pet goat so he could love on it. One day, he ran to see her, but she was not there. He searched and searched for her. Later that day, Noah and the family were served dinner by the Queen. After Noah had eaten more than half his meal, the Queen spoke with the notorious grin.

"Noah, you want to know where your goat is?"

Noah said that he had looked everywhere for her but could not find her.

"Well, that's because you are eating her," the Queen viciously replied.

Noah immediately rushed through the door to the outside crying and threw up. The Queen and Mr. Black just sat there and laughed at him. I was now more than ever ready to fight that demented, straight from Satan, Queen. I was no match for this psycho, but I was ready to be trained. I could not loss the image of little Noah so devastated by the meanest, most cruel and brutal people you could ever imagine. I cried for hours and wondered just how bad the abuse had really been. I was sure they held back some things because they had been threatened, too.

J. T. decided he would record what the boys shared. He assured me I could use the tape in court. He was now in training to be a police officer and of course he was full of knowledge and advice for me. My attorney insisted that the judge would want to hear from the boys for himself.

"No, they have been through enough," I said.

My attorney explained that the judge would speak to the boys in his chambers with him present, but I could not be there. I decided they could use the tape to hear what the boys needed to say. The judge in no way would budge on the matter. I was adamant that the boys not be brought into the courtroom to face Charles and the Queen. My attorney assured me that would not happen. My attorney had all the documentation and depositions, all the evidence and notes that I had collected. He demanded more money, a substantial amount of money, to continue the case that had already started. I felt many times since the day Charles' attorney had walked out of my attorney's office that my attorney now worked for Charles. But at this point what could I do.

Once again, I turned to Mama and Daddy. As I left my attorney's office, where I had gone alone, I saw J. T. talking with my attorney's assistant, Ms. Ruth. They were just chatting away, smiling and laughing. What was he even doing there? It was apparent to me as I stood and watched, it was not their first time to meet. That should have been another warning sign for me. At that point in my life, I trusted no one. I kept what I had seen to myself. I quickly learned just how deceiving people could be, especially those that had been adopted by the Queen and invited to perform in the play on her stage. That was only the beginning for me.

A couple of weeks before the custody hearing date, it was time for Charles' weekend visitation. I was at work and received a call from the Queen.

"Sandra, I thought you should know that Charles is taking the boys away in his airplane. I do not know where. The weather is severe, and I begged him not to take them. I placed a crash survival bag for them in their bags."

The Queen loved doing this to me. She even had a sound of excitement in her voice as she shared her concern. I envisioned that smile across her face. She had certainly not made this phone call to help me, but to stress me to my max. She thoroughly enjoyed pushing me as close to the edge as she could. I instantly left work and rushed as quickly as I could to the airport where Charles kept his plane. It was nowhere in sight. I ran to the control tower office as the wind increased and the sky darkened. She hadn't lied about the severe weather. Thunder boomed and lightening flashed. I opened the door to the office and the wind snatched it from me. It was all I could do to bring it back to nearly closing. I prayed. God, please keep my boys safe. The man behind the desk came to my aid as I struggled with the door. He pulled me inside and closed the door behind me.

"How can I help you, young lady," he asked. He could see that I was addled, almost panicked with the increasing bad weather and the thought of my boys not being safe.

"Do you know Charles Black?"

"You just missed him, a woman and two children."

"Where were they going?"

"I have no idea," he said as he looked out the window. "Charles wouldn't file a flight plan. I tried to tell him no way would I risk flying in this weather, but he just grinned at me, boarded his plane and took off."

I could no longer restrain my emotions. I thanked the man with my tears streaming down my face.

"I am sorry," I wailed. "But those are my children on that plane!"

"No need to apologize, Ma'am. I understand." He touched my shoulder briefly. He was very compassionate as if he understood my fear. I hurried back to my car through the pelting rain. A clap of thunder and flash of lightning overhead made me curl myself up as to save my own life. I made it to my car and sat there praying protection over my boys. Would I ever see them again? Where were they going? And why wouldn't Charles file a fight plan for their safety if something did happen? I cried hysterically.

After a few minutes, the rain let up a little and I regained my composure. I knew I had to return to work. I had no choice. I had lost so much time from work due to the court case and my supervisor was not at all understanding. I could not afford to lose my job. As I entered the hospital and headed speedily to my unit to finish my shift. It was readily apparent that I was frantic. I could hardly wait for my shift to end. I had noticed J. T. waiting in the distance on my return. It was not long before he had made his way up to my unit. He asked where I had gone and what was going on. So, being out of my mind with worry, I spilled my guts to him.

"I'll talk to you later."

He went on to make his rounds as if he was in a hurry to do something. At the end of my shift, I headed home as quickly as I could. I hoped for a phone call from my boys. I paced until I was exhausted. I lay down beside the phone. Just the thought of my boys needing to use a crash bag was overwhelming. I could not bring myself to even get up out of bed. I could not stop crying. I was off from work for the next few days, so I did not have to worry about that. I was emotionally exhausted.

Two days later, J. T. showed up at my house. He told me that the boys were fine, and he had located them at a hotel at Disney World. They would be calling me in a few minutes. I never questioned how J. T., a security guard, found them. A few minutes later the phone rang, and it was Alex and Noah. I completely fell apart at the sound of their voices. Thank you, Jesus. They spoke for only a moment. The woman with them let them call while Charles had stepped out. I was so grateful for that.

"I love you, Alex. I love you, Noah," I said with hot tears burning my cheeks. "Don't you ever forget how much I love y'all. I'll see you soon. I love you both."

Just to hear their little voices was such a relief. I counted the minutes until they returned to me. I knew the Queen had sat on her throne and enjoyed the torment that I experienced. It was as if I could feel her stern gaze as she watched me. Somehow, she seemed to know everything.

Forty

It was time to raise the curtain for a special day of entertainment that Charles and the Queen had composed. My attorney and I entered the court room. It seemed to be filled with people I had never seen before. It amazed me that people would waste their time just sitting and listening to other people's business. Had the Queen arranged that to also intimidate me? Across the aisle sat Charles and the Queen. Both were exhibiting their vicious shining grins.

Everyone stood as the judge entered the room. He was one of Charles' aunt's favorite judges. I had long heard of their affair. He was a very stern faced, heavy set, short older man. My mind wondered to my boys. I thought about how frightened they must have been meeting the judge based on the way he looked as a person. He absolutely showed no compassion, as he called for Alex to be brought to the stand. I immediately stood in protest.

"You promised me this would not happen!" I shouted.

I had to cry without tears. Alex was such a strong child and very protective of me. I had told both Alex and Noah to tell the truth to any question asked of them and we would be fine. I was enraged at the thought that

Charles and the Queen were so blood thirsty that they would stoop so low to put the boys on the stand. I trembled all over. I could no longer tolerate what was happening. I stood again in protest.

"They don't deserve this," I said sternly. "Please, do not do this to my children."

The judge immediately ordered the bailiff to escort me out for contempt of court with the next outburst. The judge questioned both boys. Alex testified that Noah got a whipping every weekend with the black utility belt that his dad wore to work.

"What did Noah do to get a whipping?" the judge asked Alex.

"Nothing, they just whipped him," Alex said as he shrugged his shoulders.

The judge made brutal accusations against Noah about his behavior and indicated that maybe he deserved to be whipped every weekend. As the boys were being questioned, Charles and the Queen sat with their smiles lit up like Christmas trees. How could they do this if they really cared anything at all about the boys? How could they? I was beyond frustrated, almost to my breaking point. I knew I had to fight and stay strong, no matter how critically wounded I felt. I felt as if my heart was bleeding, the pain was unbearable. I wanted to rescue my boys and run out of the courtroom. After they were dismissed, the bailiff led the boys out of the courtroom right by me. They looked at me as if I had violated the most sacred promise that I had ever made to them. Would they ever trust me again? Their little faces plastered with sadness and fear snapped me back to the raging war ahead. The Queen was so confident that this little maneuver would secure the destruction of my relationship with my boys and destroy my entire world.

I felt completely alone. Mama and Daddy were outside the courtroom in the waiting area, along with fourteen other witnesses that would testify for me, including the psych doctor from Atlanta. I quivered at the thickness of evil that had surrounded me at the mystery house, as it wafted throughout the courtroom, from my own attorney to the judge to Charles and of course, the Queen. Without a doubt, a conspiracy existed which involved all of those members.

I pulled myself together. My name was called and I marched to the stand. Charles' attorney questioned me first, then the Queen's attorney questioned me. I was surrounded like prey by a pack of coyotes ready to take it down piece by piece until it was completely lifeless. My focus remained on my boys. I would not break! I would not fall down and whimper! Accusation after accusation of untruths were released like rabid teeth grabbing at my soul. Evil seeds were thrown on hardened ground. I was determined to remain calm. I meditated on the thought that God knew how much I loved my boys. Mama had prayed, and I knew God heard a grandmother's prayers. My goal was to get to my boys as quickly as possible. For three long hours, they drilled me trying to get me to explode in front of the judge. Only by the grace of God, I remained composed. At the end of my questioning, the judge made an announcement before calling for a recess. The judge stated that J. T. had coached the boys into saying things and that he used leading questions. I had sensed a very strong dislike for J. T. from the judge. I was informed later that the judge and he had prior issues concerning the judge's son. J. T. conveniently forgot to share that bit of information with me.

"It is hereby determined at the discretion of the Court that certain evidence presented by the Defendant, namely a taped recording of the Defendant's children, is inadmissible and rejected as entered into evidence," the judge stated for the record.

As soon as the gavel hit, I went straight to my boys. I explained that they had tricked me and had promised me that they would not bring them in to be questioned like that. Alex and Noah stood together and hugged me tightly.

"It's okay, Mama," their sweet voices sang in unison.

"Oh, please forgive me," I pleaded, with tears no longer hidden.

"We love you, Mama."

With tears spilling over my beaming smile, I reassured them everything was going to be okay. I hoped they believed me.

While on break, Daddy and I stepped to an area underneath a stairwell that led down from the upper floor. I was so filled with disgust at what they had done to my boys. Daddy just held me as I could not stop shaking. Unexpectedly, a door at the top of the stairs opened with a loud creaking sound as though it was stuck and hard to open. The building was ancient and in bad need of renovations. Two men stepped out onto the landing at the top of the stairs out of our line of sight. It was my attorney and the judge. They were having conversation about the case.

"I've made up my mind," the judge stated in a low tone. "I'll grant custody of the boys to Charles. I don't care for that J. T. Dakota. Never have."

None of my fourteen witnesses had even been heard at this point. I could see tomorrow's headline: CORRUPTION IN THE COURTHOUSE. I could not believe what I was hearing. My attorney cleared his throat.

"Okay," was his deft response, as though he was Charles' attorney.

That conversation was totally against the law in the first place. Those two were not to be discussing anything in private about the case at this point. It was all I could do to not charge up the stairs and make my presence known. Daddy was livid. He kept me quiet until the two men were gone. Daddy was shaking. He walked around and explained to Mama—who was taking care of Alex and little Noah—that he and I would return in a few minutes. We needed to run an errand.

My attorney's office was within walking distance of the courthouse. Daddy and I were waiting there without an invite when my attorney arrived. Daddy expressed to my attorney in certain choice words what he thought of his behavior. Daddy quoted what was said on the stairs between him and the judge, which by the way was totally illegal with the case in motion. My attorney stood up from his chair behind his desk.

"You are a Jezebel," he shouted in a loud voice and pointed at me. "Just like in the Bible. You don't have enough money to fight Mr. Black. The best thing you can do is pack your bags and leave this town. You'll never get your boys."

By that point, Daddy and I were both on our feet. Daddy lunged across the attorney's desk, grabbed him by the shirt and pulled that sack of bull halfway across the desk.

"You will not talk to my daughter that way," he snarled through gritted teeth.

He had plenty more words to describe that attorney in his impassioned moment of anger. I pulled at my Daddy's shirtsleeve begging him to come with me.

"I need you, Daddy," I asserted. "This sick man will have to answer for his crime another time."

Daddy let go of him, and we started walking out of the office. He stopped abruptly and turned back, pointing his finger at my attorney.

"Just so we're clear," he shouted. "You're fired!"

Great. Right in the middle of the case, I was without an attorney.

"I am, as of right now, putting a lean against your case file," the attorney yelled. "That file contains all the evidence and depositions that you need to continue the case."

I was distraught to say the least. Daddy kept apologizing to me for losing his temper. He felt like he had stressed me to my max. I was worn and pale, but one thing I knew I for sure. I could not lose my boys and live.

My attorney had obviously phoned the judge immediately. Daddy escorted me back to the courthouse where the boys were, and he left again. I filled Mama in on what had occurred. Meanwhile, Daddy had gone to see an old friend, a very well-known attorney that was not part of Charles' aunt's conspiracy ring. Daddy's attorney friend agreed to help me. He and Daddy had grown very close throughout the years. Since my fired attorney had called the judge about their conversation on the stairs, there seemed to be an adjustment in the judge's attitude.

When J. T. heard what had transpired, he sent word to the judge. Just a little reminder of a secret they shared about a corrupt act involving the judge's son. I was not aware of any of these dominoes falling as I re-entered the courtroom to continue without an attorney. Everyone stood as the judge entered. He announced that my fourteen witnesses would not be called to testify. My heart sank. My witnesses had been waiting since eight o'clock that morning. How was I to win my case if they could not testify for us? I did not have access to the case files and documented evidence collected, because my attorney would not give them to me. Charles and the Queen had no witnesses. Their strategy for winning was intimidation and corruption.

Mama had prayed without ceasing.

To everyone's surprise the judge made another announcement.

"I am dismissing this case with prejudice. It is permanently dismissed. No matter the circumstances, it cannot be brought back to court by the Plaintiff. This case is done." He stood, struck the gavel, turned and walked out.

I was ecstatic, even though I was fatigued emotionally and physically. I had prepared my doctor friend, who was to be a witness and was already there waiting, in case we needed to carry out our plan. Our plan was not the one we leaned on that day. I thanked God. I was so grateful that Daddy had come through for me and my boys again, and for Mama's direct line to a faithful God.

"Daddy," I smiled up at him. "What happened to change the judge's mind?"

"Oh, just a little attitude adjustment, Baby Girl." He hugged me and kissed my forehead.

I quickly gathered my boys and thanked all my witnesses for their support, and we went home.

That last-minute attorney remained my attorney for years to come. A couple of days after the hearing, I begged my new attorney to quickly file with the court a revision of visitation with a supervised program. I was so fearful of what Charles and the Queen would do and say to my boys after they had testified. The attorney did as I had asked. But the court refused and stated that I would be arrested if I kept the boys from visiting. I was terrified for my safety and that of my boys.

Forty-One

Meanwhile, for the past two years J. T. had been attending the police academy. He now wore the badge of a cop. Along with that came a much more aggressive, controlling behavior toward me. He threatened to set up my friends by planting drugs in their vehicles. He burned me with cigarettes if I didn't give him the answers he wanted when he asked about my whereabouts. He began to be very forceful about staying at my house, even when I did not want him to.

    I had made plans to see the Righteous Brothers Concert at the Fox Theatre in Atlanta with my very best friend, Ethel. We had been more like sisters for many years. J. T. was so jealous that he threatened to hurt my friend if I didn't cancel our plans and give her ticket to him. A doctor friend had given me the tickets at no cost. I did not get to do things like that because I simply did not have the funds. I was so excited and of course, I wanted my best friend Ethel to go with me. She had been through everything with me. Even though there was so much I could not share with her, she was a true friend. With a smile on his face, I felt that he thought he had just destroyed the only true friendship I had. I had been through so much, not to mention what my boys had been through. That man's behavior mimicked Charles' behavior. He had become like a leach. He wanted to control my every move. It seemed for me that one storm just rolled over into another storm of worries and battles that never seemed to let up.

It was the weekend and time for Charles' visitation. This was the first time after court that the boys were to visit their dad. I explained to the boys that even though they did not want to go, they had to because of the court ruling. I assured them I was just a phone call away. If they needed me, I would be there. As usual, the Queen was the one to arrive to get the boys. I hesitantly led the boys to her car and told them I loved them. She acted as if she had won a trophy. She made a remark about my boyfriend the cop.

"He can't protect you," she snidely remarked. "You are such a fool."

She slowly backed out of the drive with that grin plastered across her face. I had such a heaviness that could only be described as a deep reservation about sending the boys into such a hostile environment. I knew the Queen and she would not take lightly to what the boys had shared in court. I could not fathom the cruel abusive behavior they had endured at the hands of the Queen. What had they truly been through? I would never know for sure. I often wondered if I would ever be free of that haunting nightmare of the Queen's play. She even astonished me with the extreme to which she would go to destroy me with all her fabricated stories, even at the expense of her own grandchildren.

A few hours later just before dark, I sat alone at my kitchen table. The phone rang. It was Alex and he was blubbering.

"Mama, she is going to hurt Noah," he cried. "Come, Mama, come. Hurry."

Then the dial tone came on. I immediately hit the dial back code and someone picked up and hung up. I rushed to gather my purse and car keys to go to the Black's house. The phone rang again.

It was Alex.

"Mama, hurry! Noah is in the bathroom, and she has a nail to open the door. She is going to hurt Noah."

"I'm on my way with the police, Alex," I said to my sweet baby. "Stay with Noah."

The Queen yelled something in the background, snatched the phone away from Alex and hung it up. In a state of panic and rage, I called 911.

"My boys are in danger! I need help!"

I gave the address which was across town.

"We don't have a car to send to that area," the 911 operator responded.

I called J. T., now a policeman. He was patrolling the opposite side of town, but he said he would head that way. I called Daddy. I was on my way as fast as I could go. I replayed over and over, Alex telling me that the Queen had a nail to unlock the bathroom door where Noah was hiding. I was thrown back into a past conversation when Charles told me about the hidden nail that the Queen used to unlock the door when he was in the bathroom. Oh, God, don't let her hurt my children. Why did I let them go there? Forgive me, God. As I prayed, irrepressible tears flooded my face. I was so sick to my stomach. My baby boys did not deserve this drama. They are my innocent babies.

Daddy was the first one to make it down the dark dirt road to the mystery house. Walking toward him were two little frightened boys carrying their belongings. Pawpaw hopped out of the truck and hugged his boys.

"Are you okay? Are you hurt?" he asked the boys in a worried voice. He got the boys and their things into the truck, then drove in the opposite direction a little farther down the road from the Black's house and waited for me to arrive.

Filled with guilt and shaking all over, I snuggled my boys to my chest.

"I am so sorry this happened," I said and kissed them both. "Are you okay? Did she hurt you?"

"She told us to never come back and threw our things out the door," Alex shared with a trembling voice. "I knew you would come, Mama, so we just started walking to get away."

"Oh, I am so sorry. I won't let this happen again. I will always come no matter what, always remember that. Noah, do you understand I will always come?" I expressed strongly.

God knew long ago that Alex and Noah would need each other to help one another and I would need both of them. I notified my new attorney about what had happened.

"Even if I have to go to jail," I said. "I will never send my boys back there. Not ever!"

They rarely saw their dad on visitations, just the Queen. This was just not the way it was supposed to be. Things seemed to quieten down for a while. Charles had still paid no child support, but I was not pushing the issue as not to stir things up. I did not want his money. I would take care of my boys myself. We just wanted to be left alone. I never let my guard down, because I knew the evil demented people I had dealt with all those years. They would reappear when you least expected it. They would not catch me unprepared.

Forty-Two

Three years later, J. T., now the cop, was still around. My relationship with him was very rocky. As was normal for the hospital where I had worked now for years, rumors echoed the halls, about the unfaithfulness of J. T. Even a doctor friend of mine had come to me with news of seeing him with another woman, someone that he knew. I was ready for this relationship to end. I had repeatedly tried to get him to leave, but he was as persistent as ever to stay right where he was. He contributed nothing; he never once even took the trash out. He came and went as he pleased. It was as if I had no say so, even though it was my house. He would often threaten to hurt my dearest friends, and being a cop, he could. It seemed that he had patterned himself after the boys' dad. It was déjà vu all over again. The threats, the abuse, the mental games. It was as if Charles had cloned J. T., the cop.

The boys were now twelve and thirteen years old. They both had begun to get into trouble. They had gotten mixed up with the wrong crowd at school. They had never had a dad to help guide them, and they had never known what a real family would be like in their home. Of course, they saw the loving family that I had but they needed their own. I was working five jobs at this time trying to give my boys the things that I felt had been denied them because Charles would not pay child support. I carried so much guilt inside me about how my life had played out so differently from all my dreams I had about being a loving great mom and a wonderful life with a loving husband.

I had gone to the sheriff's department to check on something that Alex was involved in, and J. T.'s ex-wife came out to talk to me. She was now a cop, also. She greeted me with a smile and kind gesture.

"After all these years I need to apologize to you," I said to her. "I didn't know he was married."

"There is no need for an apology," she responded. "At that time, we were already in the process of divorcing. We should have lunch sometime and I'll share some things I think you would like to know."

Intrigued by that statement, I asked, "Referring to what?"

"All these years, from the beginning when your grandmother was in the ICU, J. T. was working for Charles and his mother to gather information on you. I had seen pictures that J. T. took for them. He worked as a private investigator back when he was an EMT at the hospital and that's where it all began."

I thanked her and said, "I'll call you later and set that date to meet for lunch. I'd like to hear more." I rushed as quickly as I could to my car. I sat there for a few minutes as I had become nauseated, but I was grateful that the ex-wife had shared. I was already apprehensive about the matter with Alex, but this new information topped even that. On the way home I pulled off the road and just sat pondering back over the last eight years of my life. There had been so many warning signs. Now I realized why J. T., the security guard at that time, was at every corner I turned. Why he persisted in hurriedly becoming involved in my life. Now I knew it was J. T. that had a hand in the lights being turned on when I came home from hiding, the furniture being rearranged, Charles and the Queen always being a step ahead of me and my attorney. He was also friends with my attorney's assistant. How could he have found the boys in Florida so quickly? He already knew where they were, and he set it up for them to call. They were never in Disney World. It was just another act in the Queen's play that she had composed. There were no crash kits. She deliberately used my boys to inflict pain on me for days. J. T. had even bugged my phone and placed hidden cameras in my home. He was playing both sides of the fence. The statement that the Queen had made to me rang in my ears.

"He can't protect you. You are such a fool."

He was just as evil as Charles and close to being as evil as the Queen. Seems he betrayed the Queen and Charles as well as me. I went straight home and called my two best friends to help me move his things that he had stored in my basement out on the street for the garbage pick-up. I then drove to the police station and asked a friend there if he would notify J. T. that he could retrieve his belongings, or the garbage pick-up would take them away.

"As long as you give him notice that his things are subject to trash pick-up," he said. "There is nothing he can do about it. I will see to it that he receives that notice."

"Thank you so much."

"If you need anything, let me know and I'll take care of it." My friend gave me a hug and I said good-bye.

J. T. was accompanied with two police cars, when he came by on his day off to get his things. I just stood on the porch and watched. I thought to myself, just a small number of worthless items were all that this man had to account for his whole life. He had made nothing of himself. He just deceived and took from others. A few days later, he returned and tried to talk to me about living with me again, since he had no place to go.

"Surely, you are kidding me. Right?" I laughed.

I knew I had to be aggressive in my actions because J. T. did not know the meaning of the word "no." I had realized after learning the truth about who he really was that it was clearly not my assignment to take care of this impostor who had nothing. I drew a gun on him and told him to get out of my house. He dropped to the floor and he crawled to the front door thinking I was going to shoot him.

"You are never to acknowledge in public that you've ever known me. You are scum of the earth and not worth the price of a bullet." I shouted as he continued to crawl to the door. I actually enjoyed watching him crawl like a scared little child after all he had done to me. I had grown in many ways, and I was no longer a meek, shy, trusting young lady I had been in years past. I was now hardened to all those deceitful, evil characters that had somehow invaded my world. Sometime later, I learned of J. T.'s affair with a lady not far from my house. Apparently, Charles and J. T. were cast from the same mold. They were brilliant at lying, manipulation and deceit.

As days went by, he continued to harass me with phone calls, following me and sitting outside my house watching me. He would pull his car up on my grass as close to a large picture window as he could get and try to watch me inside. I called the police time after time, but just before they arrived, he would leave. He was listening on his police scanner and knew when they were on their way. I finally had enough when J. T. pulled me over on the side of the road on my way home from dinner with a friend. He reached in the window trying to choke me, asking questions of where I'd been and who I had been with.

"You will never get rid of me to be with someone else," he threatened. "I will always find you. I promise."

Those words sounded so familiar as they echoed in my mind. I screamed for help from two men standing close by. When I got their attention, J. T.

flashed his badge then got in his car and drove off. The next morning, I went to the police station and met with the chief of police. I explained what was happening and told him I wanted to file an official report. I wanted J. T. to lose his job if he did not stop harassing me. The chief told me he would take care of it and he would assign an extra patrol car in the area around my house until this problem was resolved. He advised me to tap my own phone to record his threats and to bring the recording back to him. So, I did, that afternoon.

J. T. continued to follow and hunt me down. He pulled me and a friend over with his blue lights and flashed his badge while issuing threats to my friend. I never saw my friend again after that night, because he said he didn't want to be involved in something like that.

"That man is crazy," my friend said. "Please take care of yourself."

"I am so sorry," I said.

J. T. eventually backed off, but there were still times over the next year when out of the blue, he reappeared following me. He had contacted my attorney stating he wanted to sue me for some of my property. That of course, went nowhere. But that was his mentality. My attorney just laughed at him and advised him to move on and leave me alone.

"Sandra has kept very detailed notes on your activities when you lived with her," my attorney informed J. T. "I don't think you would want that information revealed to certain people. It would be in your best interest to forget Sandra."

He had not only betrayed me on the home front, but he had deceived those in the police world as well. And even though he thought I was naïve, I certainly paid attention enough to gather some killer information on him to use when I needed it. Truly, if revealed, this information would serve as a death warrant for J. T.

Forty-Three

I was off from the hospital and just working around my house when I received a phone call from a friend saying they knew where Charles was located. I phoned a police officer friend of mine with the information, so they could arrest him, since there was a warrant for back child support and a warrant for arson. I knew that friend would not divulge my name. Later, that evening my doorbell rang. As I opened the door, I was greeted by two investigators I had never seen before. They wanted to know if I could show them a picture of Charles. I invited them in while I looked for a picture. When I showed them the photograph, they both looked at each other.

"That's him," they said in unison. "May we keep this photo?"

"Yes, of course."

They told me that they did find him at the location that had been anonymously given earlier that day, but he had presented them with a different identification card and stated that he was not Charles. They apologized, but said the other guys that were there also said he was not Charles. So, they could not arrest him.

Shortly after that, knowing that the police were looking for him and that the court had ordered child support be taken out of his check, he changed his identity, got into his airplane and flew to Alaska. He had not paid any child support over several years and now the police were looking for him in connection with an arson case.

About a month later, I was relieved in a way when another investigator visited me to ask if I knew where Charles was. I explained a little about what I had gone through with Charles. The investigator then shared that he had traced him to Alaska, but lost him. That Charles apparently had changed his identity. He was looking for him in connection with the burning down of a building. I was more than aware that Charles was capable of such an act. Remembering back to the house fire that was deliberately set across from my house many years ago. I was convinced that he had set it as a warning. No one was ever charged with that fire. I was hoping that he would stay gone forever, but I still after all this time felt that heavy uneasiness of someone watching me from the distance. I knew that there was no way that the Queen was unaware of his location. I also knew that even though he might be far off that he would not stay away from her. I knew she was always lurking just around the corner.

I lived for many years in fear of the Queen. I never opened the knock on my door with my body in front of the door. She had shared with me how someone had shot through a door putting the other person behind the door in critical condition. And they were never caught. I often wondered if this was a plan that she might attempt and had shared it as a warning to me. After all, the Queen was brilliant at mind games. This was just one example of her ability to get into my head. She thrived on evil acts.

As the years went by, people would share with me sightings of Charles around town. I could get absolutely no help from the police in dealing with him. So, I just gave up. Two more years passed, and I was informed that Charles had been involved in an airplane crash that he was piloting near the Alaskan Bush and had not survived. I was not convinced that he had not survived. Several months later, I felt the evil aura of being watched again. I knew it was Charles. He loved to play his games and try to mess with my head. I contacted the investigator that had tracked him to Alaska. I shared with him my feelings and assured him I knew it was Charles. After a few months, the investigator came by to see me. He had kept in touch with me on a frequent basis, because he felt I was in danger. He had been on this case for a long while, and the more he found out about Charles, the more convinced he was that my boys and I were not safe.

"You are right. It could be Charles," he agreed. "His body was never recovered at the crash site. By the way, there were a lot of drugs recovered at the sight and a lot of bullet holes in the plane. Just stay aware of your surroundings," he conveyed concerned.

My two boys grew older and were not around much, though I did my best to stay in touch with them. They never fully understood that I would have never made it through the treacherous nightmare that lasted for so many years without them.

Forty-Four

I had decided to move to a place where no one would know where I was. I needed some peace in my life. I was all alone, and it seemed that every other week someone was breaking in my house and violating my privacy. I needed a place that would become my safe haven. It was not until years later that I realized Charles knew exactly where I was the entire time. I carried so much guilt inside of me wondering if the decisions I had made through the years had been the right ones trying to protect my boys and all that they had to endure. I had a lot of baggage from the abuse, and I trusted no one.

Never again would I have a relationship that I would completely commit myself to. Or so I thought. However, God had a different plan. He sent a man into my life that was my soul mate. It was a devastating time in my life once again. Daddy was dying. A man that I could never have imagined life without. Mama and I stayed beside him throughout the duration. He was our rock and we both loved him beyond measure. I was his baby girl

Then there was Jessie. He had been a longtime friend from the hospital. Out of the blue he phoned me.

"Hi, Sandra. This is Jessie," he said. "It's been a while I know, but I was told you might could help me with something."

"Of course, Jessie, if I can."

"My oldest son has gotten into trouble, and I am looking for information about a drug rehab facility because he needs help. A mutual friend had told me that you knew a lot about this subject and that you also had a prison ministry. She felt sure you might could help."

"Yes, Jessie, I have a few contacts," I replied. "I'll need a little more detail."

"Can we meet for lunch?" he asked.

"Sure, but I need to stay close to the hospital where Daddy is being treated." I shared the information that I thought would be helpful then explained the situation with my Daddy. Jessie was so kind. I remember a few days later riding down the road and my phone rang.

"Hello?" I answered in a worried daze, just having left Daddy.

"I just wanted to tell you that I'm praying for you," Jessie spoke in such a kind manner.

"Thank you. I really needed that, Jessie," I replied with a full heart.

"Let me know if I can do anything to help," he said. "I'll be in touch."

I had stayed with Mama around the clock beside Daddy's bedside because the doctors had told the family that his condition was worsening. I needed to run home and shower since I had been there for several days. Mama refused to leave his side for even a minute. While my brothers were there with Mama, I decided to hurry home and get a shower and return quickly. When I arrived home, I drove up to my gate to find it beautifully decorated for Christmas. I sat with the motor turned off and thanked God that at a time like this he had sent Jessie into my life. I had never known a man so kind, other than Daddy, of course. I opened the gate and proceeded to find a beautiful wreath hung on my door with a note attached that said, "Thought you could use a little cheering up. I always knew how much you loved Christmas."

Only a few days later Daddy went to be with Jesus. I was so lost and so grieved. Mama, my two brothers and I met at the funeral home to make arrangements. My older brother was in the same hospital as my Daddy. He was very sick and not able to meet with us. When I came out of the meeting, there stood Jessie leaning up against the front of his land rover, arms folded across his chest. I stopped and drew a deep breath. I walked over to him and without a word he reached for me and pulled me close to him and just held me. He could feel my hurt.

"If you need me, I'm here," he spoke softly.

I just nodded then walked over to join my family. He was so patient with me and allowed me to heal with time. He showed me that there was such a thing as true love and he never abused me in any way. He always held my hand no matter where we were. I loved that. Always treating me with respect, he made me feel safe. We had been friends for forty-five years. We became very best friends and married in a small, quiet, elegant ceremony. We lived happily together for ten years, then God took Jessie home to be with Him.

Those ten years were the very best years of my life. The loving, caring, laughing and sharing was amazing. We shared a love in those ten years that most people never find in a lifetime. In my eyes, God had more than made up for all the hurt and torture I had endured, when He allowed me to share my life with Jessie. He was without a doubt an answer to all my prayers.

Forty-Five

Vengeance is mine, sayeth the Lord.
    Deuteronomy 32:35

As I sat on the deck of my lake house overlooking the slow-moving water down below, I was filled with gratitude for a beautiful sun-filled day. There was a gentle breeze blowing through my white hair. I began to reminisce about all that I had endured as I sipped my morning coffee. I was so grateful for the God given strength and all the blessings I had been given through those rough and rocky years.

Looking back at even the most treacherous times, I could see that God's hand was always there and that the strength I had gained was certainly not my own. I thanked Him once again for a praying Mama and Daddy, for all my friends that had helped me, and for His love for me and His protection of my boys.

Throughout the past four years news trickled in about the other cast members. Mr. Black had passed away all alone. He and the Queen had divorced several years earlier. The Queen married a man she had been having an affair with for many years prior to her divorce from Mr. Black.

Her new husband passed away not long after they were married and left her to battle with his children over the estate. The Queen experienced a torturous demise from Alzheimer's, but even at that, she spoke of her hatred for me up until the end. The attorney who was bought out by Charles and had done me so wrong in the middle of my custody case, endured prolonged suffering at his death. As far as J. T., the cop, he lost his job at the police department and moved away. He abused the wrong girl.

I was deep in thought with a quiet smile upon my aged face, now in my late sixties, when my focus was redirected to the present.

"Good morning, Mama," he spoke with an uplifted, pleasant voice.

It was Alex. He and his brother, Noah, had come to live with me and help at the lake house. I was no longer alone. How blessed I felt as Alex joined me for a cup of coffee. Little Noah, who now stood 6 feet, 4 inches, would join us later. I had dreamed of their return for many years. Oh, the peace that I had as we laughed together, fished together, went on boat rides and just sat and talked. Both Alex and Noah could make me laugh at a moment's notice. They were my reason for living and God knew how much I loved them.

After forty years, as I journeyed back to the old home place on this particular morning, I recaptured the serenity from my younger days with the news I received earlier. Charles had died a slow, painful death from cancer. The characters of the Queen's play would no longer be able to hurt me. The nightmare had ended as the last curtain was finally drawn.

Looking back, I realized that all of my dreams from earlier on had come true. God's hand was on me the whole time. I had the most loving husband I could have ever asked for. He was my soulmate. He never abused me in any way. He adored me. I have a wonderful relationship with my two boys, who love me. I have a beautiful home that is my safe haven. I had thought that my dreams were abandoned and gone, but I came to realize that my timing is not God's timing. And with the grace of endurance, God had fulfilled all my dreams and answered all my prayers.

God had given me and my boys a way out...... with the closing of the FINAL CURTAIN CALL.

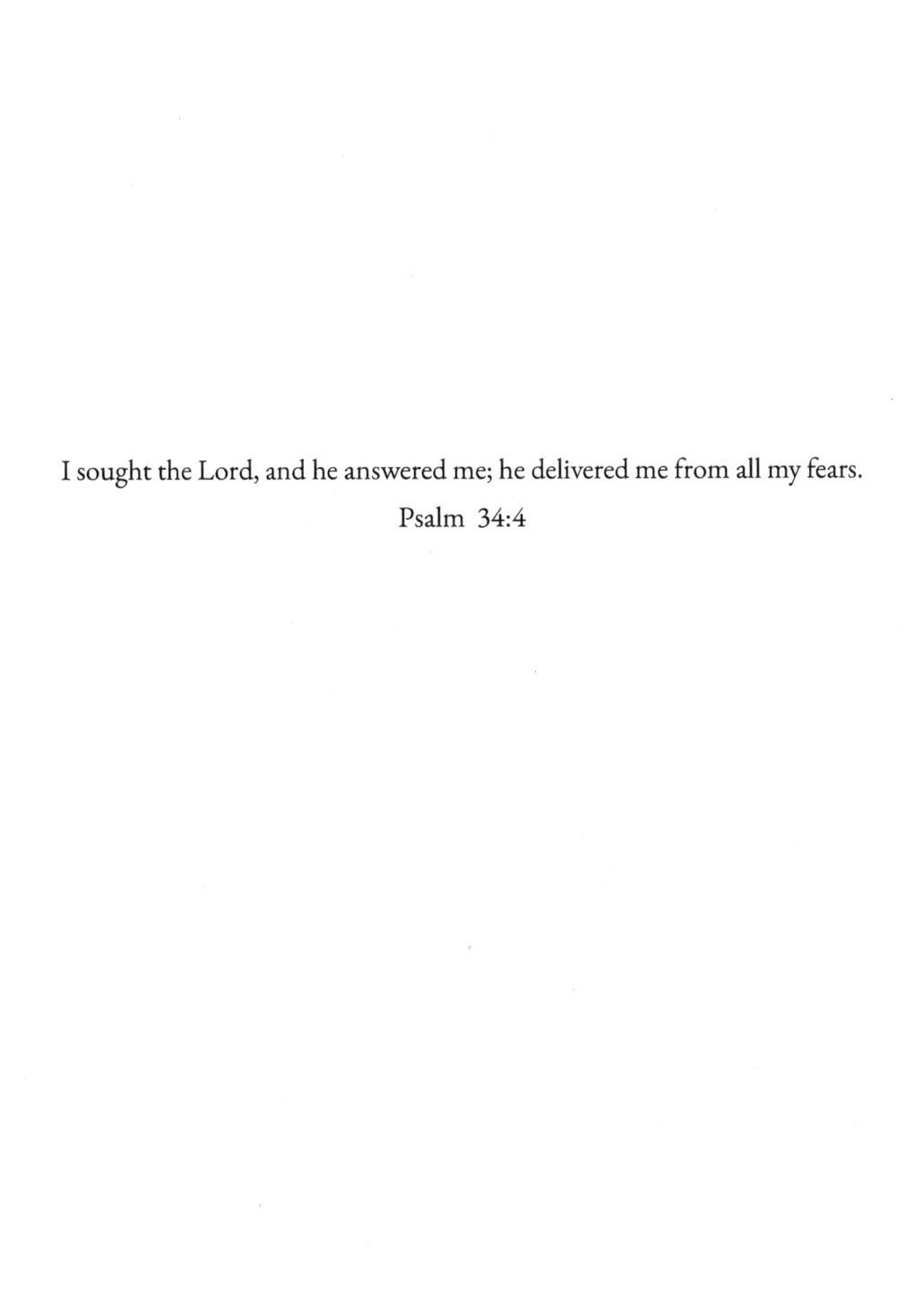

I sought the Lord, and he answered me; he delivered me from all my fears.

Psalm 34:4

Acknowledgements

My sincere and deepest thanks to the following:

First and foremost, I would like to thank Jesus for never giving up on me and giving me double in return when he restored my two sons to me.

Karli Land --- my wonderful friend and publisher who goes far above and beyond and has been such a blessing. I could not have done this without you.

Vickie McEntire ---- my awesome editor. Thank you for taking the time when you were so busy. I loved working with you.

Thank you for choosing to read FINAL CURTAIN CALL.
God bless you in whatever struggles you may have in your life. Always remember, Jesus is there.
-Rebamac
Rebamac221@gmail.com

If you are a victim of domestic violence or know someone who could use assistance in leaving a dangerous situation, help is available. Speak with someone today.

National Domestic Violence Hotline

Hours 24/7 Languages; English, Spanish, and 200+ through interpretation service.

800-799-7233

Milton Keynes UK
Ingram Content Group UK Ltd.
UKHW051000160624
443979UK00008BA/106